CHEERIO, TITAN

CHEERIO, TITAN

The Friendship between
George Bernard Shaw
and Eileen and Sean O'Casey

Eileen O'Casey

CHARLES SCRIBNER'S SONS • NEW YORK

Charles Scribner's Sons
Macmillan Publishing Company
866 Third Avenue, New York, NY 10022
Collier Macmillan Canada, Inc.

Library of Congress Cataloging-in-Publication Data
O'Casey, Eileen.
    Cheerio, Titan: the friendship between George Bernard Shaw
and Eileen and Sean O'Casey.
      p. cm.
    ISBN 0-684-19145-8
    1. Shaw, George Bernard, 1856–1950—Friends and associates.
2. O'Casey, Sean, 1880–1964—Friends and associates. 3. O'Casey,
Eileen—Friends and associates. 4. Dramatists, Irish—20th
century—Biography. 5. Authors' wives—Ireland—Biography.
6. Actors—Ireland—Biography. I. Title.
PR5366.026   1989   89-10134   CIP
822'.91209—dc20
[B]

Macmillan books are available at special discounts for bulk purchases for sales promotions, premiums, fund-raising, or educational use. For details, contact:

Special Sales Director
Macmillan Publishing Company
866 Third Avenue
New York, NY 10022

10 9 8 7 6 5 4 3 2 1

Printed in the United States of America

Permissions and acknowledgments appear on page 143.

To Breon, Shivaun, and Niall

Eileen O'Casey, 1989.

(PHOTO BY GRAHAM WOOD OF *THE TIMES*, LONDON)

PREFACE

ONCE WHEN I was very ill I began to wonder why nothing had ever been written about the friendship of George Bernard Shaw and Sean O'Casey.

This friendship meant so much to Sean. It went back to 1919 when Sean sent G.B.S. a pamphlet, *Three Shouts on a Hill*, asking him to write a preface to it. G.B.S. replied that it was out of the question, and he advised Sean "to go through the mill like the rest and get published for your own sake, and not for mine." Sean followed this advice, and actually carried the letter around in his pocketbook until it became tattered. Later, in 1926, when *Juno and the Paycock* was produced in London, Sean visited Mr. and Mrs. Shaw, who were then living in Adelphi Terrace.

Sean's friendship with G.B.S. had a great influence on him. He felt he had a champion in him, and, apart from this, there was a true and warm understanding between the two men.

The Abbey Theatre in Dublin requested that Sean send them his next play, so that they could produce it. The play was *The Silver Tassie*. It was refused by W. B. Yeats. It was a bitter disappointment for Sean, and I have written about this in detail in my previous book, "Sean." This was in 1928, and G.B.S. wrote a long and wonderful letter to Sean, praising the play, and finishing "Cheerio, Titan." From then on, until the death of G.B.S., the friendship remained as firm as ever. During the war G.B.S. lived in Ayot St. Lawrence and Sean lived in Devon so it was impossible for them to see each other, but they kept in touch through correspondence.

St. John Ervine wrote a magnificent biography of George Bernard Shaw (Sean admired it very much), but in it he made no mention of Sean O'Casey. Ron Ayling, a great friend of ours, and professor of English at the University of Manitoba in Canada, wrote to St. John Ervine, praising the biography, but asking why he had not mentioned Sean O'Casey in it. St. John Ervine replied saying he had not mentioned Sean because he did not think he was a great friend of G.B.S. He said for eighteen months he had been a neighbour of the Shaws when they lived at Whitehall Court, and when G.B.S. had visitors he liked St. John Ervine to be there because he said "he had the gift of the gab" and could keep the conversation going, which Shaw was not always able to do. St. John Ervine maintained that G.B.S. was very shy. He may have been right about this, but we did not see any evidence of it. We were always greeted with great warmth by Mr. and Mrs. Shaw. G.B.S. was completely at ease and happy with Sean, and, as for being at a loss for things to talk about, the conversation between the two men often became hilarious, each of them trying to outdo the other with sarcasm and wit. It may be that St. John Ervine was not present at any of these visits because G.B.S. knew that Sean did not like him (a feeling he shared with Lady Gregory).

All these things inspired me to write a book about Sean's friendship with George Bernard Shaw.

ACKNOWLEDGMENTS

I WOULD like to thank all the people who have helped me during the writing of this book:

The Society of Authors on behalf of the Bernard Shaw Estate for permission to use the Shaw letters, and also on behalf of the St. John Ervine Estate for permission to publish the letter from St. John Ervine to Ronald Ayling.

The Trustees of the Will of Mrs. Bernard Shaw for kind permission to publish her letters.

Colin Smythe Limited on behalf of the copyright holders, Anne de Winton and Catherine Kennedy, for permission to publish letters of Lady Gregory, and also for giving me photographs taken at Coole Park, Ireland. The Oxford University Press for kind permission to publish the letter from W. B. Yeats to Sean O'Casey.

Ronald Ayling for permission to use his letters from Sean O'Casey. The Hon. David Astor for helping me about visits from Lady Astor. John O'Riordan who spent many hours looking up detailed information about the theatre in the twenties and thirties, and who also did a great deal of research into Shaw material.

Ian Lamaison of the National Trust for giving me permission to have photographs taken at Shaw's Corner.

Wolfgang Suschitzky for taking the photographs at Shaw's Corner and permitting me to use other photographs.

Graham Wood of *The Times*, London.

The Hulton Picture Library.

The Raymond Mander and Joe Mitchenson Theatre Collection.

The National Portrait Gallery, London, for permission to use two photographs of George Bernard Shaw.

John Beary, Kathleen Doolan, Catherine Porter, and Joan Ross for their secretarial assistance.

CHEERIO, TITAN

George Bernard Shaw and Sean O'Casey, 1930.

CHAPTER
∞ 1 ∞

I HAVE wanted to write about the friendship of George Bernard Shaw, Sean, and myself for some time.

Going to visit Shaw's Corner in Ayot St. Lawrence in my later years gave me the final urge and decision. It all came back to me with such emotion—the realisation that I had lost this great friend.

This time going around the house with the caretaker, as I stood there, I was so overcome. Shaw seemed to be there in each room. I saw on the study table the picture of our family, which Shaw had asked me to give him on one of my later visits. I remembered his face lighting up as he scanned the photograph, saying, "Sean has been enriched, Eileen, with such a family, and you." He was delighted with it, and wrote Sean a letter saying what joy it had given him.

It was not an outstanding house. Years back, the first time I went to see Shaw there, I thought, as I walked up the path to the door, "What an ordinary house!" When I was shown into the sitting room Shaw greeted me with such a warm welcome. He came forward with outstretched arms, smiling, embraced me for a moment, telling me in his rich Irish voice how lovely I looked. He gave me the wonderful feeling of being with someone who *really* liked me, someone who wanted to be with me. Then I said to myself, "This is no ordinary house—this is Shaw's home."

Afternoon tea was served, cucumber sandwiches, thin bread and butter, cakes on a pretty cake stand, elegant china and a fine linen tablecloth and serviettes; those wonderful afternoon teas which we rarely see now.

Time flew by. Shaw was such a wonderful talker when he wanted to be, if he liked you. In this way he was very like my own husband, Sean. The room was pleasantly furnished. I think I remember very pretty chintz chair covers. Sitting there one looked out on to the garden. It was a large garden with great long stretches of grass and lots of trees around it, very well kept.

Then Shaw took me to see the revolving summer house which was at the far end of the garden. This was where he said he did most of his writing. I was more than surprised. I expected to see a lovely spacious summer house. Not at all. What I saw was quite a small, unpretentious little summer house. Inside there was a table with his typewriter, papers, also a telephone, a chair, a resting couch, and I did notice a small electric fire.

I realized that he must have loved the feeling of isolation when writing there. He did say to me it was his sanctuary. The view all round varied as the summer house revolved. I could imagine such rich restful countryside changing with the seasons. Spring would be full of colour; autumn, the wonderful changing leaves; and winter harsh and windy. I could visualize Shaw going down to his garden house on a winter morning, well wrapped up, entering his little sanctum, his cozy corner, with a fire on and the wild weather outside.

Now I have to go back to how I met Sean O'Casey, as it was Sean who introduced me to George Bernard Shaw.

I had been acting in America with George M. Cohan in a play called *American Born*. When the play was finished, I was in my hotel room in New York when a young girl, who had played the lead in the play, came to see me. She brought with her a play, which she wanted me to read. She was to act the leading role in it. "Can you speak with an Irish brogue?" she said. "No," I told her, "I was born in Ireland and brought up in England, and I speak the way I speak."

She left the play for me to read, and I read it from start to finish. It was called *Juno and the Paycock*, by Sean O'Casey. I was overwhelmed by it and resolved I must meet the man who had written it.

I returned to London, and I was taken to see *Juno and the Paycock* which was playing at the Royalty Theatre in Soho. Once more I was overwhelmed by the play, and was actually in tears at the final curtain. More and more I was determined to meet the writer of such a wonderful play. Mind you, I was young and hopelessly romantic.

Some days later, it was arranged for me to meet Sean O'Casey. The meeting was in the office of J. B. Fagan, the producer who had brought Sean's plays from the Abbey Theatre in Dublin to London.

That day, all those many years ago, is forever impressed on my memory. I was very nervous. When I entered Fagan's office two figures were sitting on each side of a large desk. J. B. Fagan, the producer, and Sean O'Casey, the playwright. Sean got up and came toward me. He sensed I was nervous and took both my hands in his to reassure me. He gave me a lovely smile, and said in his rich welcoming voice, "There is no need to be nervous." The immediate realization that he genuinely admired me put me at ease. How was I to know that this scene with Sean was going to happen years later with another Irish writer?

I had come to ask if I could play the part of Mary Boyle in *Juno* if the play went on tour. When the interview was over Fagan said he would write to me. I felt Sean's great attraction to me. I knew he was very reluctant for me to leave.

Two days later Fagan sent for me again. This time he told me

The Summer House, Shaw's Corner.

(PHOTO BY WOLFGANG SUSCHITZKY)

that *Juno* was coming off, but that another of Sean's plays, called *The Plough and the Stars*, was in rehearsal.

The young girl who was to play the part of Nora had been taken ill, and Sean thought I might take the part. I was to take it until Kathleen O'Regan returned, then stay on to understudy her.

I read the play. I liked it even more than *Juno*, but play the part of Nora? "No, I couldn't do that!" I felt I had not enough experience. Sean said he would go over the part with me. I knew it was a wonderful part. I suppose Sean must have been infatuated with me. Also Fagan was in a fix as he could not get a well-known actress to accept the terms of playing the part until Kathleen O'Regan's return. The play was actually in rehearsal. So Sean and Fagan persuaded me, and I said "Yes."

The rehearsals were very difficult indeed. I, inexperienced, with such experienced Irish actors and actresses as Sara Allgood, Maire O'Neill, Arthur Sinclair, Sydney Morgan, etc. It was an exceptionally difficult part, but Sean stood by me all the time.

It was a very fine opening night and undoubtedly a success. I played the part for three or four weeks. I knew I was improving each evening, but when Kathleen O'Regan came back to take the part, I, perhaps foolishly, packed up my makeup and left. I could not bear to understudy the part I had grown to love.

I got a part in a musical comedy called *The Street Singer*, touring the outer London music halls twice nightly, doing a song-and-dance routine with a comedian.

I met Sean quite often. He telephoned me every night, after I had been out dancing with my young boyfriends, mostly telling me that none of them were worthy of me! He wrote me wonderful letters.

Barry Jackson sent for me to do an audition for the part of Minnie Powell in O'Casey's *The Shadow of a Gunman*. I got the part.

This time I was not as frightened or nervous. I was absolutely delighted. Here I was back with the Irish players at the Royal Court Theatre in Sloane Square.

It meant that I saw Sean daily. I had a flat in Baker Street one side of Hyde Park, and Sean lived on the other side, in Chelsea. We met each day in the park and walked together. Sean told me of his early days in Dublin. He talked about people who had influenced him, among them Eugene O'Neill, of course Shakespeare, and George Bernard Shaw. He told me about a letter he had written to G.B.S., asking him to write a preface for a small early work called *Three Shouts on a Hill*. Shaw had replied:

10 Adelphi Terrace W.C. 2
3 December 1919

Dear Sir

I like the foreword and afterword much better than the shouts, which are prodigiously overwritten.

Why do you not come out definitely on the side of Labour & the English language?

I am afraid the National question will insist on getting settled before the Labour question. That is why the National question is a nuisance and a bore; but it can't be helped.

Of course the publishers will publish it with a preface by me; but how will that advance *you* as an author? Besides, my prefaces mean months of work. I am asked for prefaces three times a week. It is quite out of the question. You must go through the mill like the rest and get published for your own sake, and not for mine.

You ought to work out your position positively & definitely. This objecting to everyone else is Irish, but useless.

In great haste—I am busy rehearsing.

G. Bernard Shaw

This letter became one of Sean's most valued possessions. He carried it around with him in his pocketbook for years, until the edges got frayed and torn. He considered it was wonderful advice, which he followed.

Now my friendship with Sean became more intense. Sean was in love with me, and I was carried away by this man, so different in every way from anyone I had ever met. I began to see Sean every evening, instead of going dancing. Sean used to stress, over and over again, how as well as being lovely, how intelligent I was. Well, believe me or not, no one had stressed my intelligence before—always how pretty I was and flattering me. I often think this is what really won me over!

During our walks in Hyde Park, Sean spoke with great enthusiasm about a new play he was writing called *The Silver Tassie*, a war play. When Sean was telling me about this play he told me how the whole idea was nurtured. One day Sean was sitting in the office of Billy McElroy, a coal merchant who financed the transfer of Sean's plays from the Abbey Theatre, Dublin, to London. These two men became friends. In fact, Bill McElroy, Augustus John, and Sean were to be seen together almost daily in those days.

One day Sean was sitting in Billy McElroy's office. While idly sitting there, Billy started humming, and then the words began to trickle through. It was an air Sean had never heard before, a Scottish air. He cocked his ear to listen, and the words came huskily to his ear:

Gae fetch to me a pint o' wine
An' full it in a sulver tossie
That I may drink before I gae
A service to my bonnie lossie.
But it's no the roar of sea or shore
Was mak' me langer wish tae tarry;
Nor shout o'war that's heard afar—
It's leavin' thee my bonnie lassie.

In his own autobiography Sean says how this romantic song haunted him. He hummed it in his tiny flat in South Kensington; he hummed it in the dead of night, strolling down the Cromwell

Road. Yes, he decided he would give the title of the song to his play. He would set down without malice or portly platitude the shattered enterprise of life to be endured by many of those who, not understanding the bloodied melody of war, went forth to fight, to die, or to return again with tarnished bodies and complaining minds . . . and he would do it in a new way. There was no importance in trying to do the same thing again, letting the second play imitate the first, and the third the second. He wanted a change from what the Irish critics had called burlesque photographic realism, or slices of life. Yes, this is what he determined to do.

Singing had a great influence on Sean's writing. I remember later, after we were married, when Sean finished a play he always wondered despairingly how in the name of God he would ever write another line, and whatever else he could do to keep his family. The deep depression might last a week or more, but when an idea for a new play was born, I always knew it because suddenly he would start humming endlessly or singing a song—in Sean's case an old Irish air. It seemed his thoughts flourished when he was singing.

I remember one day when Sean was talking to G.B.S. about this, G.B.S. said, "Yes, I know the utterly desperate feeling of what on earth can I write about now?" But far worse to G.B.S. was when after a time, the ideas would come flooding to his mind, and he would panic, thinking, "Can I ever get them down on paper?"

Lennox Robinson of the Abbey Theatre in Dublin came to Sean asking him to be sure and send his next play to the Abbey for production. Sean was delighted about this (he had a love for the Abbey), and it certainly gave him great joy to know that he had a definite theatre which would produce *The Silver Tassie*.

After the run of *The Shadow of a Gunman*, Sean and I decided to get married, and we married in September of 1927 at the Catholic Church of the Holy Redeemer in Chelsea. We went to Dublin for our honeymoon. I was overwhelmed with excitement about visiting Dublin, the city I had left as a child of three or four years. The city Sean had left but a year or so.

Eileen O'Casey. 1926

(PHOTO BY JANET JEVONS)

Sean and Eileen on their wedding day,
23 September 1927.

CHAPTER
 2

MY FIRST impression of Dublin was not good. When we arrived in Dun Laoghaire it was a dull grey day, damp cold and drizzling with rain.

Sean had booked us an hotel in Howth, outside Dublin. A lovely hotel with a view of the ocean. We were greeted with great warmth. There was a beautiful coal fire in our bedroom, and I cheered up immediately.

We used to go to Dublin each day on a small train, and not stay in Howth. Later Sean decided we would move to Dublin.

Sean took me all around the city . . . to the galleries, the museums, and to Trinity College where he was shown the Book of Kells. Sean was not shown one page only, he was privileged to be shown two pages.

We visited Glendalock, and its famous lake, outside Dublin. He took me to the Silver Strand, a magnificent stretch of silver sand beach, and many other places.

Most evenings we would go to the theatre.

We stayed in an hotel called the Russell, which was then quite an inexpensive hotel. Later it became one of the most fashionable hotels in Dublin, with a very fine chef and dining room. It is now demolished. We moved from the Russell to the Standard, which was on the other side of Stephen's Green. This was a charming family hotel where on coming in from the theatre late at night one was welcomed by a fire glowing. At any late hour one could be served with a drink or a pot of tea. This was where Lady Gregory used to stay when she came from Coole Park, and Sean remembered visiting her there.

Lady Gregory was a founder of the Abbey Theatre and the woman behind the Irish literary renaissance. When Lennox Robinson returned one of Sean's early plays, *The Crimson in the Tricolour*, Lady Gregory wrote a letter to Sean which was sent with the rejection. She wrote, "I believe there is something in you. . . . Your strong point is characterization." Encouraged by this, Sean persevered, and in 1923 the Abbey accepted his two-act tragedy *The Shadow of a Gunman*. This play was an immense success, playing to full houses, but not on the first two nights. After the people had read the reviews in the newspapers, and word went round, not only was the house full, but people were being turned away.

Barry Fitzgerald, the famous Irish comedian, was often around with us in the evenings. We would go to the theatre, or sometimes just dinner and talk. Sean and he would bubble over with their sense of humour, overlapping each other in their sarcastic Irish mocking of various Dublin characters, from the Lord Mayor down. I was so happy in this wealth of humour. Sad to say, the Russell has also been completely demolished.

Then there was "Jammet's" famous restaurant in Dublin. Michael Scott, the well-known Dublin architect, and Doctor Cummins, who had been Sean's eye specialist when Sean was in Dublin, both entertained us there.

It was a restaurant with great personality—the waiters in their long white aprons, fine linen tablecloths, good silver and glass, excellent food and wine. The walls were filled with photographs signed by actors and actresses, singers, dancers, and opera stars. Because in the era of the twenties, Dublin was one of the most fashionable cities to visit. It had the best of theatre, opera, and dance performing there. All of the artists performing in these places would have dined at Jammet's. Now Jammet's has also gone. I think a steak house is in its place.

Our honeymoon, which was to have lasted three or four weeks, went on to six or seven. I could sense Sean's restlessness to be back to his writing. He was endlessly scribbling in his notebook which he always carried with him. Yes, we must get back to London. Home we must go!

Now Sean and I must really share our lives together.

II

On our return to London we stayed in Sean's small flat on Clareville Street, a very attractive neighbourhood. The flat was very small, just two rooms and a small kitchen, and an enormous bathroom, which, I take it, had been a conservatory. Sean's desk was under the window in the front room, which looked out on to a road with an avenue of trees. *The Silver Tassie*, the play he was working on at the time, was written at this desk.

This was a stirring and wonderful time in my life. I was completely without having to look for work. We were very content with each other's company.

Sean talked of all he had done since first coming to live in London. He talked a lot of George Bernard Shaw, and told me he had visited Shaw, the great sage, and his wife Charlotte, when they lived in Adelphi Terrace. How nervous he was to meet Shaw and Charlotte. When he entered the house, Charlotte had welcomed him with such warmth. He was lonely at the time, coming from Dublin where he had been all his life. Charlotte, he said, gave him the same feeling of understanding he had felt in the company of Lady Gregory.

When leaving Adelphi Terrace after one of his visits, he had strolled around the neighborhood for hours feeling the atmosphere where so many great people had lived . . . Garrick, Pepys, Turner. He said that even Peter the Great had once spent time there.

We chatted for hours about plays and theatre; plays he had seen. Once a week we would go to the music halls, such as the Chelsea Palace, the Holborn Empire, or the London Palladium. Sean loved music halls. He loved the slapdash humour and talent of the old music hall turns. In fact, one sees its influence in his own comedies.

We saw such music hall turns as:

Harry Tate	*—wearing his exaggerated long moustache*
Little Tich	*—in his enormous long boots*
George Robey	*—with a bowler hat and shiny, fake nose*
Florrie Forde	*—singing comedy songs*
Gracie Fields	*—the Lancastrian comedienne*
Arthur Lucan and Kitty McShane	*—as old Mother Riley and her daughter Kitty*
Harry Lauder	*—singing Scots songs*
Will Fyffe	*—singing "Glasgow Belongs to Me"*
Marie Lloyd	*—performing her witty, risqué songs*
Rob Wilton	*—as Mr. Muddle-Combe*
Will Hay	*—as the Schoolmaster and the fat boy*
Maidie Scott	*—wheeling the baby in a pram, singing "If the wind had only blown the other way, I might have been a single girl today."*

I was so surprised when Sean mentioned *Rose Marie*, as I had been in the chorus of this musical before going to New York. He said how he had admired the wonderful chorus of the "Tom Tom

*Sean and Eileen at the flat
in Clareville Street around the time Sean
was writing* The Silver Tassie *(1928).*

(COLLECTION OF EILEEN O'CASEY)

Totem Pole" song and dance, for which the chorus each night had such enormous applause.

When I told him that I had been one of the Totem girls in the chorus, he was amazed and said, "Of course . . . I remember you told me that you had been in chorus when you first came to see me at Fagan's office about acting in my plays. That lovely, wonderful day we first met."

Sean had finished his play, *The Silver Tassie*, and sent it earlier to Lennox Robinson at the Abbey Theatre. He was full of excitement looking forward to its production. In a letter Robinson replied:

Dear Sean,

Your play arrived this morning. Three cheers! I shall read it as soon as possible and send it on to Lady Gregory.

Very busy now over *Borkman*, and a new *Murray*.

Yours ever,

Lennox Robinson

How delighted Sean was to receive this letter. He also sent the play to George Bernard Shaw, as promised.

CHAPTER

3

I WAS having my first child. So, after a lot of consideration, as the flat was so small—only two rooms—we decided we would look for a larger flat or small house.

We found a house on Woronzow Road, St. John's Wood. A charming Georgian house on a road lined with trees. At the gate of our house, number 19, was a luscious laburnum tree. There was a small garden in front, and steps up to the door. It was a semi-basement house with a large front room with French windows opening on to a lovely walled-in garden. Very well kept. Magnolias, many lovely flowers, lilac bushes, trees, shrubs, and an apple tree.

We loved our house on Woronzow Road, our home. We furnished it with furniture from my flat in St. Andrew's Mansions, Baker Street, where I had lived before I was married. Also Sean's furniture from his room in Dublin, including his desk, chair, and sofa.

I was hopelessly extravagant with money. I bought modern prints from Zwemmer's on Shaftesbury Avenue, and Sean's great friend, Billy McElroy, rashly opened an account at Heal's, a very fine furnishing shop in London. We chose our curtains and carpet regardless of money. Ah well, they wore well, and were to be cut and reshaped many, many times during our married life. Looking back, it seemed to pay to buy the best, "even regardlessly."

At about this time, Sean was most anxious for me to see Shaw's *Back to Methuselah*, which was playing at the Royal Court Theatre. The play had an amazing cast including Ralph Richardson, Edith Evans, Gwen Frangcon-Davies, Cedric Hardwicke, Laurence Olivier, Eileen Beldon, Frank Pettingel, and Colin Keith-Johnston.

In those days going to the theatre seemed to be filled with excitement, and much more glamour. There was a very wonderful exhilarating feeling as one entered the foyer. Sitting in the stalls, waiting for the curtain to rise, there was a great sense of occasion. The air seemed to be electrified and tense. This is how it felt to me. Now it seems less exciting.

It was a long version of *Back to Methuselah*, which meant it lasted several hours, starting very early with an interval for dinner. I remember the evening so well because I was very pregnant, an enormous size. We sat in about the fifth row of the stalls. My feet were killing me so I slipped off my shoes. When I tried putting them on again my feet had swollen like two balloons. I had to walk to the restaurant with my toes somehow in the shoes—doing a sort of shuffle.

It was a first-class production, and I did enjoy the play. Sean had seen many of Shaw's plays at the Abbey Theatre in Dublin. Also, when he came to London, he told me of seeing Sybil Thorndike in *Saint Joan*, and what a truly great performance it was. Much later in our lives, when we had moved to Torquay, Sybil visited us. In fact she became a lifelong friend of Sean's.

Sean went to the theatre a good deal, as well as the music halls. We saw many fine productions, but performances I particularly remember were Robert Lorraine in Strindberg's *The Father*, and also in *Cyrano de Bergerac*; Edith Evans in *The Beaux Stratagem* as Mrs. Sullen, and in Congreve's *The Way of the World* as Mrs. Millamant; Ralph Richardson in *Back to Methuselah* as I have mentioned.

I saw the revival of *Pygmalion* with Cedric Hardwicke, and also his performance as King Magnus in Shaw's *The Apple Cart*, in which Edith Evans played Orinthia.

We also went to see *The First Mrs. Fraser* with Marie Tempest, I do remember extremely well, in 1930. We saw the Habina Players in *The Dybbuk*, brought over by Sidney Bernstein, and this was a fantastic piece of theatre. They wore masklike makeup, and Mary Ellis played the girl kissed by the devil. They also did a wonderful performance of *A Midsummer Night's Dream* in mask makeup.

The Barretts of Wimpole Street, with Cedric Hardwicke and Gwen Frangcon-Davies was another great performance by both. Then again Mary Ellis and Basil Sydney in O'Neill's *Strange Interlude*.

II

I was not at all easy in pregnancy. I would stay awake half the night. We used to play card games; Sean made endless cups of tea until at last I went to sleep. Gosh—he was so patient, we did laugh a lot.

I was to have my baby at home. There were complications and a specialist was called. Sean was sent away to stay with a friend, Billy McElroy, for the night. Dr. Harold Waller, my doctor, telephoned him in the early hours of the morning to tell him that he had a son, and we both were doing well. Of course he was overjoyed.

When he returned home, his letters were on the hall table. He noticed there was one from the Abbey Theatre. He told me afterward how excited he was to see this letter, but the news was anything but exciting. It said that W. B. Yeats and the Abbey Theatre had rejected his play, *The Silver Tassie*.

82 Merrion Square, Dublin
20 April 1928

My Dear Casey,

Your play was sent to me at Rapallo by some mistake of the theatre's. It arrived just after I had left, and was returned from there to Dublin. I found it when I myself reached Dublin four days ago. Enclosed with it were the opinions of my fellow-directors, but those opinions I shall not read until I have finished this letter; the letter, however, will not be posted unless their opinion concurs with mine. I had looked forward with great hope and excitement to reading your play, and not merely because of my admiration for your work, for I bore in mind that the Abbey owed its recent prosperity to you. If you had not brought us your plays just at that moment, I doubt if it would now exist. I read the first act with admiration. I thought it was the best first act you had written, and told a friend that you had surpassed yourself. The next night I read the second and third acts, and tonight I have read the fourth. I am sad and discouraged. You have no subject. You were interested in the Irish civil war, and at every moment of those plays wrote out of your own amusement with life or your sense of its tragedy; you were excited, and we all caught your excitement; you were exasperated almost beyond endurance by what you had seen or heard as a man is by what happens under his window, and you moved us as Swift moved his contemporaries. But you are not interested in the Great War; you never stood on its battlefields or walked its hospitals, and so write out of your opinions. You illustrate those opinions by a series of almost unrelated scenes as you might in a leading article; there is no dominating character, no dominating action, neither psychological unity nor unity of action, and your great power of the past has been the creation of some unique character who dominated all about him and was himself a main impulse in some action that filled the play from beginning to end. The mere greatness of the world war has thwarted you; it has refused to become mere background, and obtrudes itself upon the stage as so much dead wood that will not burn with the dramatic fire. Dramatic action is a fire that must burn up everything but itself; there should be no room in a play for anything that does not belong to it; the whole history of the world must be reduced to the wallpaper in front of which the characters must pose and speak. Among the things that dramatic action must burn up are the author's opinions; while he is writing he has no business to know anything that is not a portion of that action. Do you suppose for one moment that Shakespeare educated Hamlet and King Lear by telling them what he thought and believed? As I see it, Hamlet and Lear educated Shakespeare, and I have no doubt that in the process of that education he found out that he was an altogether different man to what he thought himself, and had altogether different beliefs.

A dramatist can help his characters to educate him by thinking and studying everything that gives them the language they are groping for through his hands and eyes, but the control must be theirs, and that is why the ancient philosophers thought a poet or dramatist Daimon-possessed.

This is a hateful letter to write, or rather to dictate—I am dictating to my wife—and all the more so because I cannot advise you to amend the play. It is all too abstract after the first act; the second act is an interesting technical experiment, but it is too long for the material; and after that there is nothing. I can imagine how you have toiled over this play. A good scenario writes itself; it puts words into the mouths of all the characters while we sleep, but a bad scenario exacts the most miserable toil. I see nothing for it but a new theme, something you have found and no newspaper writer has ever found. What business have we with anything but the unique?

Put the dogmatism of this letter down to splenetic age and forgive it.

W. B. Yeats

Sean's sense of disappointment must have been shattering. He knew he had written a very fine play.

He came to see me and our son. It was the most beautiful morning, and I was gloriously happy. Sean did not spoil my happiness by telling me of the rejection of the play, in fact he did not tell me until about a week later.

We called our son Breon.

*The old Abbey Theatre
before it was destroyed by
fire in 1951.*

(HULTON PICTURE CO.)

CHAPTER
⚜ 4 ⚜

THE WHOLE of our lives was so dominated by this rejection of *The Silver Tassie* that I feel I must give not only G.B.S.'s letters, but the whole correspondence.

The refusal and following letters became embedded in our lives at this time. It seemed as if Sean found it hard to dwell on any other thoughts. Our house was now filled with mixed emotions—distress about *The Silver Tassie*, but joy over having Breon, which helped Sean and me greatly. Dozens of letters arrived in the post. The telephone was ringing all day long. Because although Yeats had rejected the play, many others thought it was wonderful. When the papers were discussing the rejection, it caused almost a turmoil of argument, especially from Ireland where Sean was bitter and honest in his replies to the Irish press.

Sean had always been interested and involved in the Lane pictures being returned to Dublin Art Gallery. The pictures were a collection of Hugh Lane, Lady Gregory's nephew. Hugh Lane had a remarkable gift. He had what I call "X-Ray Eyes": he would be able to discover under dirt and varnish over a painting, a masterpiece. He would have it cleaned and authenticated, and then sold.

With this money, Lane went to France and lived very modestly. He bought French Impressionists which were then very reasonable in price. He wanted to leave his collection to Ireland. He also wanted the Irish government to build a gallery worthy of his paintings. They repeatedly said yes, they would, and did nothing.

In order to hurry them up, he made a will leaving his collection to the National Gallery of London unless the Irish found a gallery by a certain date, but he confided in Lady Gregory that he had no intention of doing this, that it was only a ruse in order to make the Irish government get a move on.

He most certainly would leave his collection to Ireland whether they built the gallery or not. Unfortunately, coming back from the U.S.A., he went down with the *Lusitania* before changing his will.

The Irish didn't comply with the terms of the will, so the National Gallery claimed the pictures. This was their legal right although morally, they belonged to Ireland. "And the Lane pictures became a national issue."

Sean had written several letters to Lady Gregory about this. She replied, and her letter also included the criticism of *The Silver Tassie*.

Coole Park, Gort, Co. Galway
27 April 1928

Dear Sean,

I did not answer and thank you for your very kind letter about Hugh Lane's pictures—and saying you would come to Coole again some time, (as I still hope you and your wife will do) because I didn't like to say anything about the play until W.B.Y. had seen it. His letter has only come today, and I think I ought to mail it to you at once though I am afraid it might hurt—or at least disappoint you—(as his criticism did me, on my first draft of *Sancho*). But it is right you should at once know what he—what we all—feel and think—I won't make any more comment—I know you will prefer this to any attempt to "soften" things and will believe that I, that we all—feel you would rather have the exact truth than evasions—

Yours very affectionately,
A. Gregory

The first letter of praise about the *Tassie* was from George Bernard Shaw, which read:

4 Whitehall Court, S.W. 1
19 June 1928

My dear Sean,

What a hell of a play! I wonder how it will hit the public. Of course the Abbey should have produced it—as Starkie rightly says—whether it liked it or not. But the people who knew your uncle when you were a child (so to speak) always want to correct your exercises; and this was what disabled the usually competent W.B.Y. and Lady Gregory.

Still, it is surprising that they fired so very wide considering their marksmanship. A good realistic first act, like *Juno*, an incongruously phantasmic second act, trailing off into a vague and unreal sequel; could anything be wronger? What *I* see is a deliberately unrealistic phantasmo-poetic first act, intensifying in exactly the same mode into a climax of war imagery in the second act, and then two acts of almost unbearable realism bringing down all the Voodoo war poetry with an ironic crash to earth in ruins. There is certainly no falling-off or loss of grip; the hitting gets harder and harder right through to the end.

Now if Yeats had said "It's too savage; I can't stand it," he would have been in order. You really are a ruthless ironfisted blaster and blighter of your species; and in this play there is none righteous—no, not one. Your moral is always that the

Irish ought not to exist; and you are suspected of opining, like Shakespeare, that the human race ought not to exist—unless, indeed, you like them like that, which you can hardly expect Lady Gregory, with her kindness for Kilkartan, to do. Yeats himself, with all his extraordinary cleverness and subtlety, which comes out just when you give him up for a hopeless fool and (in this case) deserts him just when you expect him to be equal to the occasion, is not a man of this world; and when you hurl an enormous smashing chunk of it at him, he dodges it, small blame to him.

However, we can talk about it when we meet, which I understand is to be on Thursday next week. This is only to prepare you for my attitude. Until then,

Cheerio, Titan

G. Bernard Shaw

This was when Sean and G.B.S. really became close friends. G.B.S.'s admiration for Sean's work gave Sean such strength. On the telephone they spoke to each other frequently. Their wit and sarcasm were perfectly matched. If only tape recordings were then available!

G.B.S.'s letter restored Sean's conviction that he had written a good play. He replied to Yeats's letter:

19 Woronzow Road, St. John's Wood.
Dear Mr. Yeats,

There seems to me to be no reason to comment upon whether you read my play in Rapallo or Dublin, or whether you read my play before or after reading your fellow Directors' opinions, or whether the Abbey owed or did not owe its prosperity to me—these things do not matter, and so we'll hang them up on the stars.

And we'll send into exile for the present the "dogmatism

and splenetic age," and have a look at the brood of opinions these have left behind them.

You say—and this is the motif throughout the intonation of your whole song—that "I am not interested in the Great War." Now, how do you know that I am not interested in the Great War? Perhaps because I never mentioned it to you. Your statement is to me an impudently ignorant one to make, for it happens that I was and am passionately and intensely interested in the Great War. Throughout its duration I felt and talked of nothing else; brooded, wondered, and was amazed. In Dublin I talked of the Great War and of its terrible consequences with Lady Gregory when I stayed in Coole. I have talked of the Great War with Doctor Pilger, now the cancer expert in Dublin, who served as surgeon at the front. Only a week before I got your letter I talked of the Great War to a surgeon here. And yet you say I am not interested in the Great War. And now will you tell me the name and give me the age and send me the address of the human being who, having eyes to see, ears to hear and hands to handle, was not interested in the Great War?

I'm afraid your statement (as far as I am concerned) is not only an ignorant one, but it is a silly statement too.

You say "you never stood on its battlefields." Do you really mean that no one should or could write about or speak about a war because one has not stood on the battlefields? Were you serious when you dictated that—really serious, now? Was Shakespeare at Actium or Philippi? Was G. B. Shaw in the boats with the French, or in the forts with the British when St. Joan and Dunois made the attack that relieved Orleans? And someone, I think, wrote a poem about Tir nan og who never took a header into the Land of Youth. And does war consist only of battlefields?

But I have walked some of the hospital wards. I have talked and walked and smoked and sung with the blue-suited wounded men fresh from the front. I've been with the armless, the legless, the blind, the gassed and the shell-shocked; one with a head bored by shrapnel who had to tack east and tack west when before he could reach the point he wished to get to; with one whose head rocked like a frantic moving pendulum. Did you know "Pantosser," and did you ever speak to him? Or watch his funny, terrible antics, or listen to the gurgle of his foolish thoughts? No? Ah, it's a pity you never saw or never spoke to "Pantosser." Or did you know Barney Fay, who got field punishment No. 1 for stealin' poultry (an Estaminay cock, maybe) behind the trenches, in the rest camps, out in France? And does war consist only of hospital wards and battlefields?

You say: "You illustrate these opinions by a series of almost unrelated scenes as you might in a leading article." I don't know very much about leading articles, though I may possibly have read them when I had the mind of a kid, so I don't quite get your meaning here. And do you know what you are thinking about when you talk of leading articles, or do you know what you are talking about when you think of leading articles? Surely to God, Mr. Yeats, you don't read leading articles!

I have pondered in my heart your expression that "the history of the world must be reduced to wallpaper," and I can find in it only the pretentious bigness of a pretentious phrase. I thank you, out of mere politeness, but I must refuse even to try to do it. That is exactly, in my opinion (there goes a cursed opinion again), what most of the Abbey dramatists are trying to do—building up, building up little worlds of wallpaper, and hiding striding life behind it all.

I'm afraid I can't make my mind mix with the sense of importance you give to a "dominating character." God forgive me, but it does sound as if you peeked and pined for a hero in the play. Now, is a dominating character more important than a play, or is a play more important than a dominating character? You say that "my power in the past has been the creation of a unique character that dominated all round him, and was a main impulse in some action that filled the play from beginning to end." In *The Silver Tassie* you have a unique work that dominates all the characters in the play. I remember talking to Lady Gregory about *The Plough and the Stars* before it was produced, and I remember her saying that *The Plough* mightn't be so popular as *Juno* yet *The Plough* is a better work than *Juno* and, in my opinion—an important one—*The Silver Tassie*, because of, or in spite of, the lack of a dominating character, is a greater work than *The Plough and the Stars*. And so when I have created the very, very thing you are looking for—something unique—you shout out: "Take, oh, take this wine away, and, for God's sake, bring me a pint of small beer."

It is all very well and very easy to say that "dramatic action must burn up the author's opinions." The best way, and the only way, to do that is to burn up the author himself. What's the use of writing a play that's just as like a camel as a whale? And was there ever a play, worthy of the name of play, that did not contain one or two or three opinions of the author that wrote it? And the Abbey Theatre has produced plays that were packed skin-tight with the author's opinions—the plays of Shaw, for instance.

Whether Hamlet and Lear educated Shakespeare, or Shakespeare educated Hamlet and Lear, I don't know the hell, and I don't think you know either.

Your statement about "... psychological unity and unity of action ... Dramatic action is a fire that must burn up everything but itself ... the history of the world must be reduced to wallpaper in front of which the characters must pose and speak ... while an author writing he has no business to know anything that isn't a part of the action ..." are to me, glib, glib ghosts. It seems to me they have been made, and will continue to be spoken forever and ever by professors in schools for the culture and propagation of the drama.

(I was nearly saying the Gospel.) I have held these infants in my arms a thousand times and they are all the same—fat, lifeless, wrinkled things that give one a pain in his belly looking at them.

You say that after the first and second acts of *The Silver Tassie* there is . . . nothing. Really nothing? Nothing, nothing at all? Well, where there is nothing, where there is nothing —there is God.

Turning to your advice that I should ask for the play back; that I should tell the press that I want to revise it, and so slip aside from the admonition of the Abbey Directorate, I refer you to what I have written already to Mr. Robinson.

I shall be glad for the return of the script of the play, and a formal note of its rejection. —Best personal wishes,

S. O'Casey

Sean was eagerly awaiting Yeats's reply to his letter—he could think of nothing else—wondering how Yeats would answer each point. On the ninth of May, Yeats replied:

Dear Casey

I have just had your letter. I write from the Abbey, Lady Gregory, Lennox Robinson, my wife & I are here for *The Plough and the Stars*—a packed enthusiastic house. Had my admiration for your genius been less, my criticism had been less severe. I think that is true of Lady Gregory and Robinson also.

Yours,

W. B. Yeats

It seemed impossible to me that Yeats could dismiss Sean's letter which had been written so meticulously point by point in

William Butler Yeats,
Irish poet and playwright, 1939.

(HULTON PICTURE CO.)

defense of his play. Would he not be any more sensitive to a fellow playwright?

On the first night of *The Silver Tassie* at the Apollo on 11th October 1929, Lady Gregory wrote the following:

Standard Hotel (Dublin)

Friday - 11th October 1929

Dear Sean

I have only just realised that your play comes on tonight —and though I never send telegrams on such occasions I want you to be sure that you have all my good wishes for it—and its success. I hope to see it myself very soon for I cross to England on Monday—I shall be for some days with Mrs. Phillimore—1, Upper Phillimore Gardens. And I look forward very much to a visit one afternoon if you invite me—to see and make acquaintance with your wife and your son—and your garden—

Now good bye—with affection—

A. Gregory

Sean replied to Lady Gregory:

St. John's Wood
15 October 1929

Dear Lady Gregory—

Thank you ever so much for your kind wishes towards the London production of *The Silver Tassie*.

The production has made my mind a-flood again with thoughts about the play's rejection by the Abbey Directorate, & bitterness would certainly enter into things I would say about W. B. Yeats, & L. Robinson if we were to meet; bitterness that would hurt you, and I am determined to avoid hurting you as much as possible.

Recently I have had to make four English papers contradict statements attributed to W. B. Yeats, that were made—it was said—at a House Party on a wet, Irish night, in a place called Kilbride, Kilcurragh, Co. Wicklow. And before me is another contradiction of a statement made by an American Literary Journal about the "naturalism" of *The Silver Tassie*. So, knowing how I feel, & guessing what I would say about the many Artistic & Literary shams squatting in their high places in Dublin, I feel it would be much better to set aside, for the present, the honour & pleasure of seeing you & talking with you.

Affectionately Yours.

Sean

Lady Gregory was obviously longing to see Sean as she wrote immediately in reply:

Dear Sean,

Your letter has grieved me—perhaps I deserve that—but I do ask you to change your mind and allow me to come and see your wife—and the boy, and the garden, and the pictures, and *yourself*. I do not feel that much pain. I am here but for a few days ('til Saturday). Could go tomorrow afternoon—if you give me leave.

As always affectionately,

A. Gregory

Sean was extremely stubborn over this—in no way could I persuade him to see Lady Gregory. I kept trying to tell him that he was only hurting himself, as deep down, he must have longed to see her. I myself wanted very much to meet Lady Gregory.

Thirty-four years later when David Krause was collecting Sean's letters, Sean remarked on his rereading this:

That was one letter I should never have written, especially that cruel last sentence, to my poor Lady Gregory! But I suppose my wounds were still raw and I wasn't strong or wise enough to forgive and forget.

After seeing the play, Lady Gregory wrote to Sean:

> (England)
> Thursday, 23 October 1929
>
> Dear Sean
>
> Although I have missed the pleasure of seeing you, I should like to tell you what I have just written to Yeats about the *Tassie*—"I am troubled because having seen the play, I believe we ought to have accepted it. We could not have done the chanted scene as it is done here, it is very fine indeed and impressive." But I say, and think, we could have done the other acts better—Barry Fitzgerald was of course very fine.
>
> I leave for Dublin tomorrow, just passing through London. I have had some pleasant days with old friends but am sorry not to have made the acquaintance of that "kid" whose father shows such splendid vitality and of his mother. I have done a little work about the Lane pictures and have great hopes of them now—
>
> As always affectionately,
>
> A. Gregory

It must have given Sean ease and pleasure to know that Lady Gregory had appreciated his play. Her opinion meant so much to him, and of course to know that she felt that the Abbey Theatre should have done the production. I can only imagine the terrific disappointment that she must have felt at Sean's continuing refusal to see her. I was very upset about it.

All the time during the controversy about *The Silver Tassie*, I could not believe that Lady Gregory had consented to the play being rejected—not on her own instincts. I felt deeply that she must be influenced by Yeats and Robinson.

I thought of the deep admiration and love Sean had for this lady over many years. Sealed by the production of *Juno*—the joy Lady Gregory had seeing her beloved theatre, the Abbey, filled to overflowing with this production. I also vividly remember the wonderful description Sean gave me of his visits to Lady Gregory's residence in Coole Park, Galway, and their wonderful conversations together. He was always immensely proud that she had asked him to carve his initials on the famous tree in Coole Park. Lady Gregory asked well-known people, whom she admired and liked, to carve their initials on the tree. Poets, artists, and writers were asked to do this when they came to Coole Park. In her determined and gracious way she would refuse people this honour if she did not think them worthy of it. The tree still stands at Coole Park, and is a tourist attraction.

It was to Lady Gregory he wrote, on receiving his first royalties from *Juno*, about the purchase of a bookcase and the joy of at last being able to buy some of the books he had longed for, among them special art books.

Sean's most wonderful writings are about women—particularly Lady Gregory and his mother—and since his mother had died, Lady Gregory was the one person with whom he wanted to share his success.

Sean did not like accepting awards, and when he was awarded the Hawthornden Prize, a literary prize for young writers, he wrote to Lady Gregory asking for her advice. She advised him to take the money as it would be useful to him. She herself came to London to speak on his behalf at the presentation at which Lord Oxford presided.

Lovely letters have passed between Sean and Lady Gregory. Sean describing his work, his home, his marriage, and his son, Breon. I thought after all these years, how could Lady Gregory agree with Yeats?

While writing this book, I was given Lady Gregory's journals to read. In *Lady Gregory—Fifty Years After* she mentions Sean with friendship and admiration. Reading this book convinced me that I was right in my thoughts all those years back that she really was not wanting the rejection of his play, *The Silver Tassie*.

She describes in several places her worry and concern over Sean. She mentions how she had sleepless nights, not being able to get O'Casey out of her mind.

Once again she mentions how she was speaking to Yeats about the *Tassie*, hoping he would change his mind about the rejection of the play, but that he had remained "frigid."

She also writes of a night where she lay awake counting the hours—with O'Casey on her mind.

She was the only one to send Sean a telegram on his London first night.

It was interesting to read also, that when *The Plough and the Stars* was sent to the Abbey, before its production, the arguments were very much against it. The language, the prostitute, the song that Rosie and Fluther sang at the end of act 2, and the idea of mentioning a child out of wedlock.

Yeats and Lady Gregory had stood by the production of this play against strong arguments with the Abbey management. In fact, when the riots broke out, on one of the nights of the first week, with people booing and hissing and throwing things onto the stage, Yeats stepped forward bravely and made his famous speech:

> You have disgraced yourselves again. Is this to be an ever-recurring celebration of the arrival of Irish genius? Synge first, and then O'Casey. The news of the happening of the past few minutes will go from country to country. Dublin

Autograph tree at Coole Park, April 1915.

(PHOTO BY W. F. BAILEY; COLLECTION OF COLIN SMYTHE)

has once more rocked the cradle of genius. From such a scene in this theatre went forth the fame of Synge. Equally the fame of O'Casey is born here tonight. This is his apotheosis.

I thought on reading this, how could *Yeats*, who had accepted Sean's genius in his play *The Plough and the Stars*, not see its expanse in the play *The Silver Tassie*? I thought he did Sean great harm in his rejection.

CHAPTER
❦ 5 ❧

NOW I go back to where G. Bernard Shaw and Charlotte Shaw first read *The Silver Tassie*.

> Passfield Corner,
> Liphook, Hants.
> 17 June 1928

Dear Mr. O'Casey

G.B.S. & I have read *The Silver Tassie* with *deep interest*. We are both greatly impressed by it—I am most enthusiastic—& we want to have a chat with you about it, & the whole business.

Could you, & Mrs. O'Casey come & have luncheon with us at Whitehall Court on Thursday next, the 21st, at 1:30? Do if you possibly can. We would be alone so that we talk freely (about our friends?!—*no*—about the play!)

Our flat is 130, & you come to Block 4 of the building & the Porter will send you up to us in the lift.

Hope to see you both on Thursday.

Yours Sincerely

C. F. Shaw

We are staying with the Sidney Webbs until Wednesday— so please write here.

I was thrilled with excitement for now at long last I was to meet G.B.S. and Charlotte.

Whitehall Court was a very large and impressive block of flats off Whitehall in London. When we entered the spacious entrance hall, there stood G.B.S. himself waiting to meet us. He came over with outstretched arms. It was to me the most extraordinary, uncanny sensation; a very overwhelming feeling, as if I were reliving what had happened before. Because, here was the same gesture that Sean had made to me when I first met him in Fagan's office at my interview in the hope of touring in *Juno*. Shaw greeted me with almost exactly the same words—it was like re-acting a scene in a play!

My impression of Shaw was of a tall imposing figure, with a shock of white hair, a warm smile, and a wicked twinkle in his eye. He had a rich Irish voice. It was a wonderfully warm welcome.

We went up in the lift. My nervousness had vanished and I was at ease. I knew he liked me and I had certainly fallen for him!

The room we entered was very spacious with lovely high ceilings and large windows. Charlotte, his wife, greeted us. On meeting her, my first impression was that she had a gentle personality, but even at that first meeting, I sensed a very determined and self-willed lady. Her admiration for G.B.S. shone out from her; in her speech, in her eyes, in her gestures. She was much shorter than Shaw, with a pleasantly rounded figure.

We all chattered away. Shaw was excited at the meeting of the

Shaws and the O'Caseys. He joked Sean a lot about marrying such a lovely girl.

I noticed on one side of the room there was a clavichord, an instrument one did not often see. I think Charlotte said that G.B.S. played it. She and G.B.S. must have shared a great love of music. I knew of his knowledge of music, and of his mother's great passion for it; music had governed his childhood. At one time he had been a music critic in London, writing for such papers as *The Star* and *The World*. Shaw later compiled all his own criticisms in a book called *Music in London 1890–1894*.

Lunch was served in another lovely, large room. It was a very gracious dining room. A waiter served us very delicate, well-cooked food. I did not notice Shaw's vegetarian food as each of us was served individually.

Shaw sat on one end of the table, Charlotte at the other. The table was not too large, however, and we were quite near enough to talk at ease.

The luncheon, of course, had been arranged for us to talk about *The Silver Tassie*. After some conversational talk, Charlotte turned to Sean and said, "You really must be more tactful in your replies to the Abbey Theatre and the press."

She obviously could not possibly begin to know his bitter disappointment. He had written a fine play, two years' hard work. How could he be tactful?—what an unfeeling remark.

Charlotte seemed to wish to take Sean under her wing, almost suggesting and advising him to write his letters in a less angry manner, not to argue so much and let her or Shaw advise him.

I knew this was utterly impossible. Sean had to be his own person and fight in his own violent way. Tact was not in any way part of his nature.

It was awkward for me to say this; she was much older than I, and I did feel very shy of her. Suppressed by Charlotte's rather dominant character, I did not reply as fiercely as I felt. I mildly said, "Sean could hardly not be hurt and resentful of the whole situation—particularly Yeats's attitude."

Surely Charlotte would understand this?

This seemed to break the tension, and conversation took on a lighter tone. Shaw also said to Charlotte that rejection for a work you know to be fine was very wounding and to be rational about it was almost impossible.

We talked well on into the afternoon. Sean reminded G.B.S. of the first letter he had written to him, asking him to write a preface to a small book he had written and that G.B.S. had replied magnificently with the great advice, "No preface. If they printed the article it would be because of my preface." Shaw chuckled over this incident, especially when Sean said that he had never strayed from that advice.

When we left, I felt that both Sean and I had found a firm and wonderful friend in G.B.S.—Charlotte also, in her own way. I secretly knew that I had found an admirer in G.B.S.!

On July eighth Charlotte wrote about their difficulty in coming to Woronzow Road for a while.

8th July 1928

Dear Mrs. O'Casey

I am so very sorry, but I fear we can't go & see you now because we are just starting off abroad for a holiday & have got so terribly tied up with all the silly odds & ends we have to get done before we go. We have taken our sleepers for Sunday, & are going to be down here until Thursday afternoon.

I am the more sorry for this as I do feel "Sean" wants a lot of looking after just now. He is going to be very naughty & fierce & resentful—& he is a terribly hard hitter!

That idea of letting G.B.S. see his letters to his "Friends" is a grand one. Do keep him up to it. Any letters addressed to 4 Whitehall Court will be forwarded *at once*, & I will send you our address the moment we are settled, & he must write about all he is doing, & G.B.S. will answer *quickly*, & try to act as a lightning conductor!

Directly we come back we will go & lunch with you, & see Breon, if you will ask us again.

Our very kindest & friendly thoughts to you both.

Yours sincerely,

C. F. Shaw

P.S. Mr. Yeats didn't come & see us about the play, but about the Irish Literary Academy they are trying to get up. He never mentioned *The Silver Tassie*. It was *I* who insisted upon talking about it—& he was rather self-conscious & reluctant!

I could not understand what Charlotte Shaw could be thinking of; she certainly did not begin to understand Sean. I did know G.B.S. would not want to be a lightning conductor—the whole attitude puzzled me. She seemed to want to mother Sean but I did not want her to smother him. I am sure she meant well as I know she had a great liking for him.

Sean still could think of nothing except the rejection of his play by the Abbey, and fighting for it. The thought came to him that although Macmillan Publishing Company had always printed his plays as soon as they were written, maybe they would not wish to publish the play now that the Abbey had rejected it.

He wrote to G.B.S. telling him that he had gone foot-haste to Daniel Macmillan telling him that they could withdraw their offer to publish *The Silver Tassie* if they thought Yeats's criticism more important.

29 June 1928

Dear G.B.S.—

May I send to Macmillan's the following portions of your letter to me about *The Silver Tassie*?

"What a hell of a play! . . . a deliberately unrealistic phantasmo-poetic first act, intensifying in exactly the same mode into a climax of war imagery in the second act, and then two acts of almost unbearable realism bringing down all the voodoo war poetry with an ironic crash to earth in ruins … there is no falling off, or loss of grip—the hitting gets harder and harder right through to the end."

When I got the queries of criticism from the Abbey, I galloped off to Macmillan's and told them they could withdraw the book if they thought the criticisms more important, and though they held on to the book, I feel they got a shock, so when your letter came I sent it on to cheer them up, and they have asked me to seek your permission to print some passages.

Besides, as far as I can see at the moment, the coming year must be financially filled up with whatever the sale of the book may bring in and any help in this way is a gift from God.

I confirm my assurance that I have no vindictive feeling to the Abbey—I refused four offers to have the play produced in Dublin—and that I should be glad to have *The Silver Tassie* performed there subject to conditions mentioned which, I think, are fair and just under all the circumstances.

Warm regards to you and Mrs. Shaw.

Sean O'Casey

Shaw replied, on 3 July, writing at the foot of Sean's letter:

My dear Sean,

Yes: Macmillan's may quote the passage as above.

I have just heard from Lady Gregory. I gather that she has really been on your side all through; so there will be no difficulty there.

Don't *disparage* L.R., or "make conditions." Say that he is the rottenest producer on God's earth, and would kill a play even if St. Luke and Gabriel collaborated to write it. He won't

*G.B.S. and Lady Gregory
at Coole Park, April 1915.*

(PHOTO BY W. F. BAILEY;
COLLECTION OF COLIN SMYTHE)

mind that or at least won't resent it; and the conditions will follow spontaneously.

Playwriting is a desperate trade. £300 a week for just long enough to get you living at that rate, and then nothing for two years. Your wife must support you (what is he for?) and when she is out of work you must go into debt, and borrow, and pawn and so on—the usual routine.

Such is life.

G.B.S. 3/7/28

To take Shaw seriously would be impossible for me. The way he would write in an off-hand manner, letting his humour and wit run away with him was, I think, an Irish characteristic.

Sean replied a few days later:

Dear G.B.S.

I don't see how I can save myself from imposing conditions. The whole affair has been carried out in a cloud of conceits; I am human & can't release suspicion from my mind. I know so much about the Abbey Theatre.

I'm sure the play was rejected before it was sent in. The mode & manner was no surprise to Yeats, for when he came to London he came to me to make sure the play would be offered to the Abbey, he was told of the new manner & method of the play—that it concerned itself with the G.W. [Great War] & he made no remark of remonstrance.

The first evasion was in Robinson's acknowledgment of the receipt of the play when he said "I will read it as soon as possible. Very busy now with a new Murray (play) & a Borkman production." Though I knew he had read it, & could hardly read it quick enough.

The second was Yeats's statement in his letter to me saying that he dictated his letter before "I opened the letters of the

· 48 ·

other directors," which is countered by a statement in a letter from L.G. saying "that she couldn't remember writing this letter" (though she recorded in her diary that she agreed with L.R.'s opinion).

The third was (date?) an answer from R. to a letter from me suggesting a Caste saying that he would pay attention to it; he was sending in the play to Yeats & was off in a hurry on a holiday.

The fourth was the effort made to get Lady Gregory's friendship for me to make (not for me) the rejection as easy as possible for them!

The fifth: was the determination to prevent the publication of the letters shown by AE writing & wiring to me to show his fright over the possibility of an action for breach of (copyright) against him by Yeats, & the only way I could reply to the stirring of his fourth dimensional conscience was to write saying, No, AE, "don't be trying to act the bloody Gaum!"

The sixth was the concealment from me of the one criticism [Dr. Starkie's] that was in any way favourable to me, & which possibly never would have been known if he hadn't rounded on his fellow-Directors in an interview with the Press.

How do I know these things! Ah! How did I know that Yeats was coming to London, & coming to see you before he stepped on the ship in Dublin Bay.

They have turned a Playhouse into a silly little temple darkened with figures past vitality, giving vision only to see coloured-windows of Yeats, L.G., Synge, L. Robinson and out [of] this temple what are called Abbey Dramatists step cautiously to play their little tunes of adoration on the little organ.

I feel that this letter shows the candor and truthfulness of a man who was convinced that he had written a good play and is defending it.

Sean wrote to Daniel Macmillan to suggest that as a preface to the play, the entire controversy between Yeats, the Abbey Theatre, and himself should be published. Daniel Macmillan replied:

Dear Mr. O'Casey,

We have read through your correspondence with the Abbey Theatre people with great interest, but we think that on the whole it would be a mistake to publish it in the book as a preface, so I am returning it to you. By the way, I suppose you would still like us to issue the play now instead of waiting till the autumn? We can issue it quite soon, as it is already being printed.

I am

Yours sincerely

Daniel Macmillan

The play was published in June 1928. In July, Daniel Macmillan decided to print the quotations from Shaw's letter on the dust jacket of the book. Then G.B.S. sent a letter to Lady Gregory.

(?) June 1928

Why do you and W.B.Y. treat O'Casey as a baby?

Starkie was right, you should have done the play anyhow. Sean is now *hors concours*. It is literally a hell of a play; but it will clearly force its way on to the stage and Yeats should have submitted to it as a calamity imposed on him by the Act of God, if he could not welcome it as another *Juno*. Besides, he was extraordinarily wrong about it on the facts. The first act is not a bit realistic; it is deliberately fantastic chanted poetry. This is intensified to a climax into the second act. Then comes a ruthless return for the last two acts to the fiercest ironic realism. But that is so like Yeats. Give him a job when you feel sure he will play Bunthorne and he will astonish you with his unique cleverness and subtlety. Give him one that any second-rater could manage with credit and as likely as not he will make an appalling mess of it. He certainly has fallen in up to the neck over O'C. But this is not a very nice letter, is it? Consequently the very last letter I want to send to you. So I will stop before I become intolerable.

G.B.S.

Again it was G.B.S.'s deep understanding and concern at this time that made a genuine human friendship last between these two great Irish men.

Sean sent his play, *The Silver Tassie*, both to Barry Jackson and to C. B. Cochran to ask if they would consider producing it. Barry Jackson came to see Sean. I opened the door to him. He was a rather dapper gentleman elegantly dressed, and I noticed he smoked a cigarette with a long holder. He went up to Sean's room. They were some time talking together. Then I heard Barry Jackson rush down the stairs looking very upset.

I said goodbye to him—he shook hands very hurriedly and off he rushed. He was in quite an emotional state. I then went upstairs to Sean's room. Sean told me what he had said. He thought that Sean had written the most wonderful play, but it was too frightening for him to produce.

This was a terrible disappointment to Sean. He could not see why such a producer who thought the play so wonderful had not the courage to produce it. It was a mystery to Sean, particularly because he admired Barry Jackson's work.

And then the glorious news!

C. B. Cochran wrote saying that he would produce the play. It meant that Cochran had to take time in raising the money for such a large production by finding backers. Sean was so happy. It was wonderful to think that C. B. Cochran, one of our finest theatre men in London, was to produce the play.

In his autobiography, *I Had Almost Forgotten . . .* , Cochran wrote as follows about the production of *The Silver Tassie*.

Among the straight plays which I have had the most pleasure in presenting to London was *The Silver Tassie* by that unquestionable genius, Sean O'Casey.

It was the rejection of this fine play by the Abbey Theatre management in Dublin which gave me the chance of producing it in Shaftesbury Avenue. The Abbey people were afraid of the bold symbolism of the moving wartime material culminating in that magnificent litany of the guns. O'Casey's previous plays, including *Juno and the Paycock* which I consider among the best plays of all time, had been realistic. But *The Silver Tassie* impressed me very much more, although on closer study I doubted whether we could ever secure theatrically the subtle effects intended by the author, much of which depended on the employment of chanting actors. I called in Raymond Massey, who made an admirable production, sensitive and original without being the least bit cranky. Augustus John kindly consented to provide a design for the war episode. This great painter proved the most modest artist who has ever swum in my pond. Big man that he is in his own sphere, he protested that he had no knowledge of the theatre. But he brought in many more fresh ideas than lesser artists claiming greater technical knowledge—indeed I consider that his scene was a masterpiece of theatrical design.

This production worked out admirably, for all the personalities concerned pulled together splendidly. We had a great combination of talents, for Martin Shaw arranged the chanting, and, as I have said, Massey produced and John was the designer of the big scene, and O'Casey professed himself enormously pleased with the result. After the first performance we all saw defects, but I think that these would have been evident whoever had had the handling of this difficult and subtle creative work. Some of the critics found the realism of the beginning and end of the play incompatible with the definite symbolism of the episode of the trenches. I share the author's view, however, which is that the first and last acts are by no means sheer realism. For the men return to their homes almost as spokesmen of a new order, voicing different social or moral concepts, rather than as ordinary men of an Irish town. Several speeches in the dance-hall scene, for example, are nothing if not symbolism. They do not represent ordinary conversation, but reach occasionally, as in the chorus of wounded men, great heights of symbolic poetry.

The Silver Tassie caused heated discussion among playgoers. Some thought I ought to be canonized for producing it, others thought I ought to be burned at the stake. Some short-sighted people could only see in it a pacifist diatribe against war; others accused O'Casey of maligning the British officer; others saw the play as a magnificent statement of deep poetic truth. For my part I regard it as the finest work yet accomplished by one of the greatest of living playwrights, and I look forward eagerly to seeing his next play. I would cheerfully wager that *The Silver Tassie* will stand the test of posterity's judgment.

The personal friendships of authors whose plays I have presented are the pleasanter heritages of my calling, and among these I treasure none more highly than the friendship of Sean O'Casey. His beautiful wife Eileen was one of the bridesmaids of *Bitter Sweet* and more recently appeared in *Helen!*

*C. B. Cochran, the famous
impresario of the twenties.*

CHAPTER
6

OUR LIVES went on very happily. Sean was busy writing a new play, *Within the Gates*. It was about Hyde Park. Sean had been fascinated by Hyde Park ever since he came to London. Speakers' Corner, which was at the Marble Arch entrance to the park, was where speakers of all denominations stood on rostrums and held forth on every 'ism, creed, and nationality; each gathering his crowd around him. G.B.S. spoke at Speakers' Corner in his younger days. Mostly he spoke in the East End, but he undoubtedly did stand on a rostrum and hold forth in Hyde Park.

During the time when C. B. Cochran was raising money for *The Silver Tassie*, to talk over casting and other details, Sean and I used to go on Sundays to a weekend cottage Cochran had rented not too far from London. It had the most wonderful garden and swimming pool. We would go for lunch and stay until late evening. Somehow in those days summer was summer; the sun shone and I don't remember a wet Sunday.

Sean and Cochran would discuss the play with Raymond Massey, who was to produce it. On one of these occasions, C. B. Cochran spoke to me seriously about my future. He said I must go back to work. I could not in any way see why, as I had Sean and Breon. He was worried about Sean being older than I and at my age being so used to going out to supper and dances in the evenings that I might become bored. He had grown very fond of Sean, and he was really worried that I might in some way hurt him. Anyway, the result was that I went to an audition and was accepted for a part in Noel Coward's *Bitter Sweet*, which ran at His Majesty's Theatre for three years.

G.B.S., when I told him I was returning to the stage, was delighted. It meant I was earning a living! Also it was good to keep "my end up."

Now it was arranged for Charlotte and G.B.S. to come and see Breon. I invited them for tea. Well, you can understand the excitement there was in Woronzow Road. The nanny I had engaged to look after Breon, as I was returning to work on the stage, was a country woman called Nanny Trim. She was a tiny delicate lady who had spent her life looking after babies and had a real love of children.

She had dollied Breon up for the occasion—his first meeting with the great man—and she carried Breon in like a royal prince. Oh no, Breon was not impressed! He screamed his head off at the sight of this imposing figure with his great white beard. G.B.S. laughed loudly which did not help matters. He said, "Breon showed great wisdom." He was obviously delighted to see such a beautiful baby!

Breon did calm down eventually and stared in amazement very quietly at G.B.S. I feel that Breon developed a complex about Father Christmas after this day, for he always hated Father Christmas in shops as a child.

Leaving Sean and G.B.S. to talk (they always seemed to outdo each other in words), Charlotte and I took Breon upstairs, where he contented himself playing and pushing animals and toys around.

Once more I listened to intense advice as to "how to manage

The set of the play The Silver Tassie,
designed by Augustus John, Apollo Theatre, 1929.

(THE RAYMOND MANDER AND JOE MITCHENSON THEATRE COLLECTION)

Sean"! I was only in my twenties, and Charlotte, as I have said before, was much older. I had a feeling that she wanted to take me, as well as Sean, under her wing. I felt shy and unable to express myself with Charlotte, and certainly I found it almost impossible to talk about Sean's feelings at the time. She just seemed to overawe me. Anyway, deep down, I did not agree with her.

I did know about her family background, and that she came from a very wealthy family, the Payne-Townshends. She had the advantages of a good education, travelling abroad and being presented in Dublin society. As a child she was more devoted to her father than to her mother. She spent many hours in his library, reading his books, they became close companions. As a young woman she had a good carriage, red hair, and green eyes. She had many suitors but it seemed she had no desire to marry. She may have been influenced by childhood memories of her mother flying into tantrums when she could not get her own way, and her father's eventual submission to his wife's whims. She hated these scenes, and they may have been the reason she did not marry until later in her life, when she met George Bernard Shaw. She admitted to me she did not like children. It seemed we had nothing in common except we had both married great Irish writers.

We visited the Shaws quite often—mostly luncheons for about six or eight people.

Oh, those luncheons in the early days! How I used to dread the conflicts between Charlotte and Sean. Sean's stubbornness in defending himself against Charlotte, and her always telling him he was a quarrelsome man and should try to be more careful when dealing with people who had influence and mattered! And all of this, of course, said in a very polite manner.

"Why do you do it?" she said.

"Why do I do it?" echoed Sean. "Somehow or other I am made to do it. Your husband did it, and still does!"

"There you go again. You quarrelled with Yeats, you quarrelled with George Russell [AE], and now you are quarrelling with James Agate."

"I didn't quarrel with Yeats," said Sean quietly, "I differed with him on the question of drama, and I differed with Agate on his opinions."

"You see, you stay obstinate. Why do you do it?"

"I don't know," said Sean, "something within me speaks before I am aware of it." Sean was trying very hard to be good humoured, "maybe it is the promptings of what they call the Holy Ghost!"

"What do you mean by the Holy Ghost, just what do you mean?"

G.B.S. was trying very hard to ease the tension. There was a slight feeling of discomfort, and he said, in a calm, humourous voice, sitting upright in his chair, "He simply means, Charlotte, that he has got something and I have got something which you have not got."

Then I said, "Actually Sean is too honest; he says things in a blunt way. He doesn't mean to be unpleasant, he is merely truthful. I think he is right!"

During these luncheons, apart from discussions, there was much witty conversation and always laughter.

I really feel it was no animosity on Charlotte Shaw's part to rub Sean the wrong way. It was just that she was never able to understand Sean's character. Sean had also a great admiration for Charlotte in her great love for G.B.S., and the care she took of him.

Actually at this period Charlotte sent Sean a book on Blake. Sean thanked her in a letter.

Dear Mrs Shaw—

Many thanks for sending me Blake's *Vision of Job*. It was very good of you to do this. I have so far read, trying diligently to comprehend, the Notes, List, Preface & Introduction, & I have read & read the first two chapters, & looked at Illustration No. 1 & Illustration No. 2, but I am, at the end of it all, as mystified as Blake's admirers.

> *Come into my hand*
> *By your mild power; descending down the*
> > *Nerves of my right arm*
> *From out the Portals of my Brain—*
> > *Oh, Blake, Blake, Blake.*

The right hand, therefore, is connected with, Poetry, Paradise, Vision. Oh, Wicksteed, Wicksteed, Wicksteed!

But I will read the book leisurely & carefully & thoughtfully, some of the coming nights, when I sit by the fire & there isn't a mouse stirring. And it was kind of you to send it to me. Best wishes to You & G.B.S.

> Sean O'Casey

Charlotte used to say how much she admired Helen Waddell's poems. She also greatly esteemed George Russell (AE) and mysticism. Sean did not like Russell—they never openly discussed this. Sean just kept a polite silence when Charlotte went into ecstasies about him.

In Christmas of 1928, Charlotte sent Sean a present of Helen Waddell's *Medieval Latin Lyrics*, with this inscription:

> *How charming is divine philosophy!*
> *Not harsh & crabbed, as dull fools suppose,*
> *But musical as in Apollo's lute,*
> *And a perpetual feast of nectar'd sweets,*
> *When no crude Surfeit reigns.*

Yes, there really was a desire for a closer understanding of Sean on Charlotte's part—she wanted Sean to really read and love and deeply understand these poems, read and love what she admired.

There were never very young people at these luncheons—though several times Cecil Lewis and his lovely young Russian wife, Duska, were there. Cecil Lewis was working at the B.B.C. at the time. He was such a handsome and charming man. Mrs. Shaw liked him very much, and G.B.S. gave Cecil Lewis his first talking picture, *How He Lied to Her Husband*, to produce. I particularly remember this, his first film, because not only was I at the luncheon, I also, at the time, was playing one of the bridesmaids in Noel Coward's *Bitter Sweet*. Rose Hignall, one of the other bridesmaids, went to an audition for one of the parts. She was not chosen for the part, as another young actress called Vera Lennox played it. This was in the year 1931.

Once, when we were visiting Whitehall Court, Shaw greeted me in his usual warm and flattering manner. He had the painting of himself by Augustus John standing upright on a table in the drawing room: "Well, Eileen, what do you think?"

The painting was in a wonderfully sunny position and seemed to shine out in "silver and blue." I loved it. A very noble brow and the eyes farseeing—a little glint of humour in them. I don't think G.B.S. liked it, or Charlotte didn't like it, or at least they did not seem sure. Sean thought it a very fine portrait. Augustus John painted three portraits of Shaw. One Shaw kept himself; the second he gave to the Fitzwilliam Museum, Cambridge; and the third, after many vicissitudes, now belongs to the Queen.

Augustus John had given us a very wonderful wedding present of a portrait of Sean. Actually John had painted a portrait of Sean that was sold to the Metropolitan Museum of Art in New York. John had asked Sean to sit for another portrait. For this one he put a big red handkerchief in Sean's pocket. One day, when Sean and I were having tea in John's studio in Mallard Street, Chelsea, Augustus very shyly said, "I have a present for you both—a wedding present." He took us to the other side of his studio where there was a second portrait of Sean.

At Whitehall Court, the only other painting I noticed was one of Charlotte when she was younger, with green eyes, by the Italian G. A. Sartorio. When I visited Ayot St. Lawrence later, I noticed both of these paintings were there—also the Rodin bust of Shaw.

Augustus John had written to Sean earlier praising *The Silver Tassie*, saying, "your play has moved me profoundly. Lawrence of Arabia, who has been sitting for me, finds it the 'greatest thing of our time.'"

Lawrence of Arabia (T. E. Lawrence) used to visit the Shaws frequently. I thought he had a lovely personality, very shy, with a dry wit. Mrs. Shaw particularly liked him—and he her. He didn't talk much at the luncheon table, but afterward he and Sean were locked in conversation together.

Once at Whitehall Court, when Lawrence was there, the subject arose as to which was G.B.S.'s favourite play. Shaw never minded discussing his plays. Sean, on the other hand, was always very shy and nervous when talking about his work. Everyone at the table of course said *Saint Joan*! But Sean said that though *Saint Joan* was his most popular play, a wonderful and magnificent play, he felt that *Heartbreak House* was the more original, deeper, and nearer to life. G.B.S.'s face lit up, he was delighted. "I think it is my best play; Charlotte doesn't, she likes *Saint Joan*." Certainly this is most people's opinion.

Now, I was working in *Bitter Sweet*, and, as I have said, G.B.S. was absolutely delighted that I was back working in the theatre; and C. B. Cochran's production of *The Silver Tassie* was getting nearer. Raymond Massey was to direct this, and the cast was a cast of stars—Charles Laughton, Barry Fitzgerald, Beatrix Lehmann, Una O'Conner, Ian Hunter, Winnie Barnes, and Emlyn Williams. Charles Laughton played Harry Heegan, Barry Fitzgerald was Sylvester Heegan, and Emlyn Williams, the trumpeter.

In a letter to his friend Gabriel Fallon in Dublin, Sean wrote:

Dear Gaby—
    Up to the neck in the whirl & sweep of the *Tassie*'s re-hearsals. Going gloriously. Charlie Laughton's a genius. Play-

Portrait of George Bernard Shaw
by Augustus John.

(PHOTO BY WOLFGANG SUSCHITZKY)

ing Harry with amazing strength & pathos. Will's [Barry Fitzgerald] here & doing grandly.

Cochran had of course decided to do a really first class production. I had been asked earlier to approach Augustus John, asking him to do the set for the second act, entitled, "Somewhere in France: in the war zone." Though reluctant at first, he did say yes.

"Eileen, you have won me over, I will do the set." He did a magnificent set, following every detail of Sean's description.

When the curtain went up on this scene on the first night, the audience started to clap, but the effect was so beautiful that they stopped clapping and became almost silent.

Cochran's first nights were always amazingly glamorous. Red carpet. The cars would arrive one after the other, and out would step the occupants in the height of fashion, greeted by the theatre ushers. Beautiful evening cloaks, furs, jewels, very elegant gowns in silver and gold with matching shoes and evening bags on chains. Cameras were trained on all the people of note. Now the glamour of first nights seems to be limited to film premieres.

After a great deal of discussion, Cochran let me have the night off from *Bitter Sweet* for the first night of *The Tassie*, and my understudy went on. G.B.S. and Charlotte were there, of course, at the first night. Sean spent the evening standing at the back of the stalls he was so nervous. He told me later that Shaw managed to find him at the interval, after the second act. Shaw was filled with excitement, saying over and over again what a wonderful play it was.

In a letter to Charles Cochran Sean wrote:

G.B.S. was with us on Thursday, and would like to write about the play, but prefers to write to you, instead of directly to the press. So, if you still think well of this, you could ask him to write to you—or I can do so—and he will send the letter on to you, to do what you think useful with it.

And G.B.S. did write Cochran a letter which appeared in *The Times*:

4 Whitehall Court

My dear Cochran,

I really must congratulate you on *The Tassie* before it passes into the classical repertory. It is a magnificent play; and it was a magnificent gesture of yours to produce it. The high-brows should have produced it; you, the Unpretentious Showman, DID, as you have done so many other noble and rash things on your Sundays. This, I think, will rank as the best of them. I hope you have not lost too much by it, especially as I am quite sure you have done your best in that direction by doing the thing as extravagantly as possible. That is the worst of operating on your colossal scale: you haven't time to economise; and you lost the habit of thinking it worthwhile. No matter! A famous achievement. There is a new drama rising from unplumbed depths to sweep the nice little bourgeois efforts of myself and my contemporaries into the dustbin; and your name will live as that of the man who didn't run away. If only some one would build you a huge Woolworth theatre (all seats sixpence) to start with O'Casey and O'Neill, and no plays by men who had ever seen a five pound note before they were thirty or been inside a school after they were thirteen, you would be buried in Westminster Abbey.

Bravo!

George Bernard Shaw

Cochran was noted for his extravagant productions. He was a magnificent showman—Oliver Messel, the famous designer, worked for him in a number of revues.

I was still working in *Bitter Sweet*, which meant I had two matinees a week and was, of course, at the theatre every evening. Apart from this, I was doing photographic work for hats and furs and working for people like Dorothy Wilding and Janet Jevons, famous photographers in Bond Street at that time.

Sometime after *The Tassie* had closed, and while *The Plough* was playing in London, Sean wrote to Charlotte Shaw:

23 June 1930

My dear Mrs Shaw—

I was delighted to hear that you had again rallied yourself back into our ranks. I felt your fight would be a good one, & that you would get better again.

And now you must be careful of yourself—more careful than before—for a hard fight leaves a little weaker for a long time.

I suppose you did well, but did you do wisely, to go to *The Plough and the Stars*, and lose your sleep over it. Wait 'til you are quite well before you plunge into anything that will keep you from resting, besides it isn't the sick poor sinners that should be called to repentance, but the righteous that are filling the world with institutions for our physical & spiritual redemption.

Of course, my dear Mrs Shaw, I am really gratified that you and G.B.S. thought so well of the play, & of the acting by little Kitty Curling, who has talent, & who has had a pretty rough time of it in Dublin.

Don't forget to take care of yourself 'til you are quite strong again.

Give my affectionate regards to G.B.S.

Yours affectionately

Sean

Before Sean had finished *The Silver Tassie*, G.B.S. had written to Sean about the interest of Ivor Montague in making a film of *Juno*, and he wrote wisely about the film rights:

3rd March 1928

My dear Sean

I hope you don't mean you have sold the world film rights of three plays forever for £5000. However, probably that young enthusiast will not be able to produce the money in time. In that case, you should make a mental note that £30,000 pounds for five years for the three is not at all an impossible figure.

Never let a right go for ever. Five years is the limit. If the arrangement is satisfactory it can always be renewed. And be sure to have a clause that in the event of bankruptcy all rights revert to you.

Have you joined the Society of Authors? They have a film committee which ought to be able to put you up to the sort of agreement you should make.

Send along the new play by all means as soon as it is born.

Ever,

G.B.S.

The new play was *Within the Gates*. Shaw was once more enthusiastic over Sean's work. G.B.S. was always so flattering, and knowing one is admired by such a person is a wonderful uplift.

About this time, when *Bitter Sweet* came to an end, Sean had no plays running and we found ourselves hopelessly short of money, having spent our money rather extravagantly on our house. Neither Sean nor I had any idea of the value of money.

G.B.S. had insisted to me that it was impossible for a writer or artist not to be financially erratic, he was paid so irregularly. If he received a large cheque, he would spend it, not asking when the next might arrive, if at all. Rather he would look forward to the sale of a film or to the production of a play.

After a great deal of discussion, we decided we would sell the short lease of our house in Woronzow Road and move to Chalfont St. Giles in Buckinghamshire, where we rented a small cottage. So off we went, lock, stock, and barrel with the cheque we got for selling the lease of Woronzow Road.

Billy McElroy's daughter, Evelyn, had this small country cottage which Billy rented to us. It was a workman's cottage on the estate of Misbourne House. The estate had several such cottages outside the village itself

When we got to Chalfont St. Giles, it was really beautiful countryside and absolutely lovely weather. We spent our days walking miles and miles in the country, sometimes pushing Breon in his pushchair. We then thought it might be cheaper if we rented a house in Chalfont itself, and I could go on with my work on the stage by commuting. We found a bungalow in the village itself. It was a lovely old fashioned village then. In the centre was the main store, and there was a seat outside where a rather demented lad was always sitting. Geese were wandering around hissing and I was really scared of them in case they pecked at my legs.

Our bungalow was set back and had a good garden in front and an orchard at the back. Opposite our gate was the famous Milton's Cottage, a great attraction to visitors.

At this time, Sean had a letter from Charlotte:

27 August 1931

Dear Sean,

It is delightful to hear of you even with such troublesome tidings as you send. I am glad you are in the country as I know you both wanted to get away from London & it will be so good for you—and, another thing is I think you will be just within a drive of us—a long one—but unless I am

*Sean O'Casey in the garden
at Chalfont St. Giles, about 1931.*

(COLLECTION OF EILEEN O'CASEY)

very mistaken, quite a possible one. I have no Bucks maps here; we are away for a holiday, which always means rather a more busy time than usual. Of course they are all at G.B.S. to write about Russia, & he finds it rather difficult to do. He can talk by the hour, but when he starts to write he doesn't seem to know where to begin! However one article is finished now, & another is nearly done. He had a wonderful experience there, & he has got a wonderful uplift from it. They seem to be the only hope of the world just now—the Russians.

I *am* so sorry about the Broadcast. You should never tell anyone your ideas for plays, for sometimes even the best people forget they are yours, and fancy they thought of it themselves; I am so sorry, I can't remember you ever telling me anything about Hyde Park. I remember perfectly your saying you were working on a *film*, & not a play, when I last saw you because I was sorry & wanted the play. That is all I remember. Earlier than that, you told me you wanted to write about English workmen—dockers I *think*.

Dear Sean—is your play very far advanced? & will this Broadcast matter? I can't help feeling anything you write will be so original, & so different from other people's work, that nothing they do will harm you that way.

And oh! dear Sean, don't be too belligerent!

Love to you both from your friend—

C. F. Shaw

What a dear little book Lady Gregory has written about Coole.

Sean responded with:

I do not know how much I must read into your advice "not be too belligerent." God be my judge that I hate fighting. If I be damned for anything, I shall be damned for keeping the two-edged word of thought tight in its scabbard when it should be searching the bowels of knaves and fools. I assure you, I shrink from battle, and never advance into a fight unless I am driven to it. I give you a recent instance: The Abbey Theatre are going on a tour through America; notices appeared in the press, mentioning the plays, which include *Juno*. I wrote to Mr. Robinson about this, and he replied that he had asked the Chicago Lecture and Concert Association months ago to get in touch with my American agents, Samuel French, Ltd., and that they had asked for an advance of five hundred dollars; this was refused, with the statement that all the other dramatists were satisfied to do without an advance. I rang up the Author's Society, explained the situation, and was strongly advised to stress for the advance. The intimation (that the Abbey had selected *Juno*) came so recently that I had no time to write about the matter, and so to avoid any suspicion that I wished to hurt the success of the tour, I wrote to the agents telling them not to bother about any claim of an advance or royalties. So, in face of a possible misapprehension, I shrink even from insisting on a very modest demand.

On behalf of James Joyce, before me now, is a letter I received this morning, which tells me that someone has translated a story into German, and has had it published in a German paper over the name of this writer. Joyce declares that he never wrote the story, and that his signature is a forgery. And, worse than all, the thing is altogether beneath the genius of Joyce. Now should I sing silently in my heart of the meanness of this deception against an artist; or should I give this man the comfort of indignant sympathy from a comrade in the evil that has been brought upon him? I shall not keep silence, and the song in my heart and on my lips shall be in harmony with the indignant song of Joyce.

Sean had now finished *Within the Gates*, and sent it to Cochran, but Cochran could not raise the money:

My dear Sean,

I am very worried about *Within the Gates*. I don't believe I could produce it without financial loss. It is true that I might incur this with less worthy material.

You have written some grand stuff and I am intrigued by your manner of introducing the singing, although you have created another difficulty for the producing manager who must find an actress who can sing. The non-singing actress is difficult enough to find—the combination is very rare. I wish I could see my way to risk the production but frankly I can't.

I am glad you are changing the Bishop's wife to the Bishop's sister. I read your play before your letter and I felt that you were limiting what the Bishop stood for by giving him a wife. Please send your sketch, "End of the Beginning," and I might be able to place it for you, although I shan't have use for it as I am not contemplating any more revue productions.

I hope ever so much that I am wrong about your play and that somebody will do it and earn royalties for you. You can't go on writing fine things, Sean, unless they bring some material reward. I suppose you are tired of people advising you to go back to the methods of *Juno*. I wish you would.

Yours as ever,

Charles B. Cochran

Sean was indeed tired of such advice, and he replied as follows:

My dear C.B.,

Thanks for your kind letter telling me what you thought about *Within the Gates* and, alas, telling me that you couldn't take the risk of its production. Although I hadn't asked you, I, of course, had a hope that the play would appear under your name. But I clearly understand your fear, and though I have a feeling that this play stands a far better chance than stood *The Silver Tassie*, I realize that a "feeling" is a poor thing to put before any sensible Manager. But I can't see why the play, being at least above the average, should be cluttered with costly accessories, and that, since a risk must be taken, why that risk shouldn't be as simple a risk as possible, with a simple scene, and a group of actors ready to act in a good play—a play that gives each a good part—for a reasonable salary.

As regards the sketch, I have the air of a song to get, and when I have this I shall send it on. It wouldn't be suitable for any revue that you might put on, for it was written for Sinclair—who pestered me into doing it when he was out of work—and then didn't do anything with it. I have been able to afford only two elaborately typed copies of the play, and I should be glad if you could let me have back the copy I sent to you.

Your advice to go back to the genius of *Juno* might be good for me, bad for my conception of the drama. And the fault of finding it almost impossible to get a good play produced is not in us, neither in you nor in me, but in an ignorant public that have nothing, and who, eventually, shall lose even that which they have.

Please give my best wishes to Mrs. Cochran; and good luck

to you till you are in a position to do any damn thing you like.

Yours as ever,

Sean

Around this time, Samuel French offered to buy the amateur rights of *Juno*, *The Plough and the Stars*, and *Gunman* for £300, with a half share of the royalties. Sean wrote to G.B.S. telling him about this and received the following reply:

23 July 1932

My dear Sean,

Read the enclosed printed slip very carefully. It bears on the proposal to buy a third of your amateur rights. I strongly deprecate that transaction, as I have never sold a copyright nor given a license to perform for longer than 5 years at the utmost. But there is a special difficulty about amateur rights, because there is no agreement as to what the word amateur means; and you may find yourself involved in lawsuits if you give professional terms, as I do, to little local societies of poor enthusiasts whom the agent and the snobbish authors class as amateurs and demand impossible five guinea fees from because they cannot afford salaries and play for the love of art, or even pawn their shirts to pay for the hall. They take fifteen shillings at the door, or by a collection. They pay me ninepence; and I touch my hat and respectfully solicit a continuance of their custom. To expect five guineas from them as if they were idle ladies and gentlemen who fancy they can "do Gladys Cooper's part" or "Gerald du Maurier's" as well as the originals, is not only grasping and snobbish but extremely stupid, as it is these little ventures, affiliated to the Drama League, that keep the theatre alive at the roots. It would pay me to pay them to play instead of putting crushing charges on them. But if I had not all my rights intact I could not discriminate. So take care. Better retain all your rights jealously, and have your amateur fees collected by your trade union, the Society of Authors, for 5%, French charges 20%.

As to guaranteeing the Bank, why should I? An overdraft bears interest. The enclosed is shorter, cheaper, and replaceable entirely at your convenience.

Faithfully,

George Bernard Shaw

The "printed slip," *Playwrights and Amateurs*, written by G.B.S. himself, had a note written at the bottom of it.

£300 for half rights for your lifetime plus fifty years is an absurdly bad bargain for you, though it is perhaps as much as you could expect from them. My advice is to let wife and child perish, and lay bricks for your last crust, sooner than part with an iota of your rights.

Very good and sound advice! This was obviously said tongue-in-cheek, but the reality of it was that Sean had no money at all, except what he earned from his writings. I had no money of my own, except what I earned on the stage, and in fact, at this time, my mother decided to sit down and give up, and let Sean and me support her. G.B.S. did send a cheque for fifty pounds but that wasn't anything like enough to settle our debts so Sean sold the rights to Samuel French! Obviously a very rash and hopeless arrangement, but we were literally up a gumtree for money and so that was that.

Charlotte wrote at this time:

I rejoice to think of you both [she wrote on 15 November] in your own home with the garden and peace and quiet.

Only I wish you were a little nearer. We know Chalfont St. Giles quite well. We had a friend there once we used to drive over to see, only we were younger then and there were not so many cars on the road. Now I find it very hard to get G.B.S. to go out on winter afternoons. Summer, yes—he likes it—but in the winter he says, "Wait until the days are longer." So I am afraid we'll have to wait! It is because he hates these lanes after dark, and meeting cars with blazing lights in fogs round corners.

I am longing to hear you have a new play ready. Has the move interfered with one? G.B.S. has just finished his new one.

It is called *Too True to Be Good*, and I call it a "super farce"; I think you will like it.

Sean replied to Charlotte:

Chalfont St. Giles
(?) November 1931

Dear Mrs Shaw—

Thanks many times & more for your kind letter. Go away to the sun if you can for the sun is more than raiment or than meat.

Of course we wouldn't expect you or G.B.S. to come over to us on a dark &, probably, cold & gloomy afternoon. And why should he bother to take trouble to see me anyhow? And, besides, G.B.S. is never absent. He is one of my great friends, anam-chara-soul-friend, as we say in Ireland, & has been so for many years, long before I met him in the flesh.

I daresay, according to the register of Time, that G.B.S. is ageing, but in reality he is a babe and a suckling out of whose mouth cometh wisdom & understanding. And this present-day cant of youth makes me sick! A young fogey is a worse

Portrait of Charlotte Shaw
by T. A. Sartorio.

(PHOTO BY WOLFGANG SUSCHITZKY)

nuisance any day than an old fogey, & there are thousands of young ones strolling about today.

I'm looking forward to the publication of *Too True to Be Good*—it's a rare title, & contains in itself a terrible philosophy.

Should I go to London on a Thursday or a Friday—& you be there—I shall ring you up, but, if you have friends with you, or you are tired, or G.B.S. wants to be with his own thoughts, or if you should have any reason whatsoever which would prompt you to be by yourselves, you must tell me, & I shall be content to wait for a more favourable day.

Breon's in splendid condition, & is growing in strength and wisdom day by day.

I'm afraid the moving did interfere a lot with my work but it can't be helped. We were to come into where we now are in June, but the tenant stayed on till October, so we had to live in a little furnished cottage till the place became vacant. We had to use oil lamps there, & as I couldn't give up my reading, I used to place a lamp on the floor, lie down beside it, & leaning on my elbow, just do the best I could do. The interest I had in the books I read prevented me from noticing a growing pain in my elbow, & one day I found there a painful & ugly swelling. I had got "housemaid's knee" on the elbow! Surgeon said it would probably mean an operation to have the swollen sacs removed, but, when we got into our new place, I dug, hoed, rolled, fixed bookcases, cupboards, shelves, & various other things, exercising the arm tremendously & foolishly, so that now the swelling is gone & the arm is practically well again!

I began last week to get back to the play or film—or whatever it may turn out to be—& to the semi-biography to be called, *A Child Is Born*.

Love to you & to G.B.S.

Sean

Now we were kept busy because Samuel French, to whom we had sold the amateur rights of the three plays, asked us to do set plans of the plays. We both struggled through somehow. These rather straggly plans are still in the amateur paperbacks of the three plays, and I must say they look pretty awful!

As Cochran could not raise the money for *Within the Gates*, Sean had an offer from another manager (producer), Norman MacDermott. Sean phoned G.B.S. about this saying he was very unsure; he considered MacDermott to be rather a rascal and was very wary of him. G.B.S. then wrote to Sean as follows:

My Dear Sean,

I take it you know that the gentleman you mention is a desperado, and that you must not get into his hands irrevocably. He knows by experience that he cannot get credit from anyone except the author, having cracked in his former enterprise heavily in my debt. Artistic desperados are forced to be reckless, not to say unscrupulous. As they do the pioneering they are to be encouraged and helped rather than snubbed; but they cannot expect long contracts and assignments of rights. One gives them the run of the piece subject to their producing within, say, six weeks, when it appears that they have really got hold of a backer. But nothing more; no contingent rights, no firm offer; absolutely nothing but the license for the run; and even this had better not be signed until there is a pretty full understanding as to the place (theatre), cast, date, etc. If an opulent backer is probable, an advance is a good way of hurrying up production.

I thought I'd mention it. If you are forewarned, there is no harm done. If not, some good perhaps.

I do not want to disparage the particular desperado in question. He got through a tidy lot of work under impossible conditions.

Lady Anne Gregory, July 1911.

(COLLECTION OF EILEEN O'CASEY)

You will be able to size him up for yourself: he is just what you guess he is.

Ever

G.B.S.

Sean was in need of money, and he wanted his play to be produced, and so he accepted MacDermott's offer to produce *Within the Gates*.

I did return to working on the stage, first playing in the revival of Rutland Boughton's opera *The Immortal Hour*, produced by Barry Jackson. *The Immortal Hour* was based on Fiona Macleod's play about the fairy princess who weds the high king of Ireland, and who must be wooed back to her own people. It had a six-week run at the Queen's Theatre, and my luck continued, for immediately *The Immortal Hour* closed I went in C. B. Cochran's revival of Max Reinhardt's *The Miracle*.

This was an amazing production—the whole of the interior of the Lyceum Theatre was turned into a cathedral. It had a great cast—Lady Diana Manners as Our Lady; Tilly Losch as the Young Nun; and Glen Byam Shaw was also in the cast.

Quite an amazing production. I used to stay in London all week, returning to Chalfont after the show on Saturday, and coming up each Monday for the Monday evening performance.

When *The Miracle* was over, I went into another of Cochran's productions, a musical called *Mother of Pearl*, by A. P. Herbert, with music by Oscar Straus. I played an Irish barmaid and understudied the French maid "Fifi"!

It opened in Manchester at Christmas. I was heartbroken to be separated from Breon at Christmas.

Mother of Pearl then came to London to the Aldwych Theatre. It had a very short run. When it closed, I decided that I would leave the stage. I was having my second child. I realized Sean needed me to be with him. His health was not good and he was involved in his writing and needed my company, and particularly at this present time as Sean had decided to accept MacDermott's offer.

CHAPTER
❧ 7 ❧

THE PRODUCTION of *Within the Gates* went into rehearsal. This meant Sean had to be there for rehearsals, and I went with him to London. Sean was very unhappy over the rehearsals. MacDermott, who produced the show, used to hold endless cocktail parties at 6 P.M. for friends, and I presume, backers. This approach was so different from the totally dedicated producing of C. B. Cochran, where a quick cup of coffee was about all to be expected.

In London, Lady Astor offered us a small flat at the top of her townhouse in St. James's Square for our stay during rehearsals. It was an absolutely charming flat and very comfortable. What filled Sean's heart with glee was that in the bedroom a coal fire used to be lit every evening. The flat was actually her daughter's, but she wasn't using it.

I thought Lady Astor a very good looking woman. She dressed mostly in very well-tailored suits with blouses—rather business-like. She was lively and quick in movement and voice—a great deal of sarcastic humour. I liked her; she was a very domineering and impetuous person.

Lord Astor was also a very good-looking upright figure. He was not always with us for lunch or dinner, but he always joined us for breakfast and sat at the head of the table. I have never forgotten how he used to have very lovely strawberry jam with his toast. He and Sean got on well together in spite of their different political views.

Now I used to see G.B.S. quite often as he used to visit Nancy Astor for her luncheon parties. He was a great favourite of hers. I was always there at these luncheons, but Sean was not often present as he was at rehearsals. Charlotte rarely came with G.B.S. He used to be very gay, flippant, and flirtatious. At various luncheons I remember different people such as Ellen Wilkinson—then called "red Ellen" because of her shock of red hair and her very left "politics." She became the first woman minister of education in Attlee's 1945 government and I do remember Anthony Eden.

Often there was an elderly lady, very beautiful, called Miss Hamlyn, whose home was in Clovelly, Devon. I used to think she was a relative of Nancy's, as Dave and Jake, Nancy's sons, would call her Aunty; but actually she was not. Bobby, Nancy's son by her first marriage, was often there. I liked him very much. I found him charming, and he was well liked by the family.

In 1931 G.B.S. visited Moscow, during the Stalin days. Lord and Lady Astor and their son David, Philip Lothian, and Marcus Hindus were on this visit.

Charlotte and Nancy Astor were great friends, and at one of her luncheon parties Nancy was teasing G.B.S. and joking him about how she had once washed his hair on the cruise. "You are," she said, "one of the vainest old boys I have ever known." In order to keep his hair snowy white she said that she had rinsed it with white of egg—it must have needed a great deal of rinsing! I thought lemon juice was the rinse for white hair—or does that make it go yellow?

On another occasion, G.B.S. startled us all when he cut into a

George Bernard Shaw in 1929.

(PHOTO BY BASSANO. COURTESY NATIONAL PORTRAIT GALLERY, LONDON)

peach and gave a great yell! The centre was bad. He turned to Nancy laughing and said, "Well, Nancy, one would not think to have a bad peach offered in a millionaire's house!"

Once Nancy mentioned a letter she had had from T. E. Lawrence, in which in one small paragraph he had mentioned *The Silver Tassie*.

> O'Casey? Sean? Indeed yes, I have just finished his new play. The second act of *The Silver Tassie* was my greatest theatre experience, and here is a whole play in that manner. It will play better than it reads.

It was strange the friendship between G.B.S. and Nancy Astor —G.B.S. being a socialist with very definite views; and Nancy Astor a full conservative with very, very, definite views. But even more strange was the friendship between Sean and Lady Astor. Sean was extremely left in his politics, but it didn't seem to matter. They argued, but stuck to their guns. Nancy called Sean "my old red"!

The opening night of *Within the Gates* had the usual smart audience. The Shaws, Lady Astor, Lady Londonderry ... Nancy Astor gave a supper party after the opening at her house in St. James's Square. Somehow it was not really very gay, no matter how one tried. One could not help having a very flat feeling as one realized that it had not been a success. G.B.S. thought *Within the Gates* was a marvelous play, both visually and poetically, but he was distressed that it had not had a finer production.

Sean had some remarkable letters about it, one describing how much T. S. Eliot had admired it.

Nancy Astor insisted we stay on for a few days after the first night; she arranged for a car to take us back to Chalfont St. Giles. On the morning before we left she said, "Oh, Eileen, I have another letter from T. E. Lawrence which he wrote to me after he had seen *Within the Gates*."

Hat stand in hall at Shaw's Corner.

(PHOTO BY WOLFGANG SUSCHITZKY)

My Piresse,

If you see O'Casey again, before this letter grows cold, will you please bless him for me? I have seen his Park play twice, and it has cost me only half-a-crown in all. That is real kindness. I don't want to see it again, for it is too painful, despite its beauty. How far he has gone since he was in Ireland, on paper! This play in London and human (and inhuman) nature; all of us, in fact; and about as helpless. And talking of inhumanity, how dare he pile loads like these upon his actors and actresses? He asks the impossible, but he gets, I think, more than he deserves. Poor dumb laden beasts. And the poignancy of Act II, *The Tassie* is not here; it could not be, for much lay in the contrast of that act's neighbours, in the wonderful lighting and setting; in the experience which came rawly upon those new from the War. This play deals with the life we all have to lead (temporarily) and so we dare not detach ourselves from it and criticise or pass judgment. That's why I do not want to see it again. However I shall read it once more, in the peace of my own cottage, which is ever so far away from his park and equally solid too, God be praised. I was right in feeling that this play would be better seen than heard, than merely read.

Bless him again. He is a great man, still in movement. May it be long before he grows slow, stops, returns on his tracks! I have learned a great deal from him.

YOUR AIRMAN

When a rare Irishman does go on growing, you see, he surpasses most men. Alas that they are so rare.

Making for Southampton again.

T.E.L.

The play did not have very good notices, it actually only lingered for about four weeks. But an American impresario saw the production and bought the play for New York. Sean was asked to go over. This gave great joy to George Jean Nathan, the famous critic, for when he read the play he tried to get a production in America. Also Eugene O'Neill, when he read the play, had written to Sean.

15 December 1933

My dear Sean O'Casey

I have been meaning to drop you a grateful line ever since I finished reading your *Within the Gates*. It is a splendid piece of work. My enthusiastic congratulations! I was especially moved—and greenly envious, I confess!—by its rare and sensitive poetical beauty. I wish to God I could write like that!

All who admire your work here—and there are a lot of us!—are hoping the play may be placed with the right management to give it the New York production it deserves. And when it is produced I hope you may come to this country and that while you are here you and Mrs. O'Casey will find time to visit Mrs. O'Neill and me in our home in Georgia.

I have just seen the English edition of *Within the Gates* and I deeply appreciate your generous reference to *Mourning Becomes Electra*. If anything about that play has suggested anything which was of the slightest service to *Within the Gates* I am only too flattered and I like my trilogy all the better for it!

Good luck to you! My admiration for your work—and all personal good wishes!

Eugene O'Neill

P.S. For years, every time I've read a new play of yours, I've meant to write to you to this same effect—and my only excuse for not having done so is that where letters are concerned, I'm the laziest man on earth!

Now all was concentrated on getting Sean ready to go to New York for the production of *Within the Gates*. I was not going as I was having my second child. Also, only Sean's fare was being paid, and certainly there was not enough money for my fare!

In America *Within the Gates* had a first-class production at the National Theatre where it opened on 22 October 1934. Lillian Gish played the young whore, and Melvyn Douglas directed it.

Apart from the fact that the play had a very fine production, Sean was so happy and loved New York and America. He met and spent many hours with George Jean Nathan, Brooks Atkinson, Richard Watts (the theatre critic), and Eugene O'Neill, all of whom became his friends for life. I did regret, deeply, not seeing this production in New York!

All through the autumn of 1934, Sean wrote me glowing letters about the success of *Within the Gates*. He absolutely loved America. This seemed very odd to me that he should have taken to New York as he did. G.B.S. must have ben thinking about Sean at this time, for in a letter to Lady Astor, about *Within the Gates*, dated 9 February 1934, he wrote:

> Sean O'Casey is all right now that his shift from Dublin slums to Hyde Park has shown that his genius is not limited by frontiers. His plays are wonderfully impressive and reproachful without being irritating like mine. People fall crying into one another's arms saying God forgive us all instead of refusing to speak and going to their solicitors for a divorce.

Within the Gates was to have been produced in Boston, but the cast arrived to find that the play had been banned. What a very odd coincidence it was that on the day of Breon's birth the Abbey Theatre rejected *The Silver Tassie*, and on the day of Niall's birth, 15 January 1935, Boston banned *Within the Gates*!

On his way back from America, Sean visited W. B. Yeats in Dublin. They talked of the Abbey and how the theatre needed new life through a new type of play, and how several new directors had been added to the board to create a better variety of opinion. During this conversation, Yeats suggested that Sean had suc-

George Bernard Shaw at his desk in 1937.

(PHOTO BY STUDIO LISA. COURTESY NATIONAL PORTRAIT GALLERY, LONDON)

ceeded in the dialogue and technique with *Within the Gates*, where he thought he had failed in *The Silver Tassie*. It went through Sean's mind that this was in fact an excuse for the rejection of his one play by the praise of another! Yeats told Sean that he would like the Abbey to put on *Within the Gates*. Sean didn't want to refuse this, but pointed out the difficulties of this production. He didn't think the Abbey stage could accommodate the play's action. He suggested they do *The Silver Tassie*, a far easier venture. Yeats paused over it and said he would consider it.

Indeed some time after Sean's return to our home in London, the Abbey Theatre produced his *Silver Tassie* in Dublin, seven years after it had seen the lights of London.

CHAPTER
8

S OMETIME BEFORE Sean went to America for the production of *Within the Gates*, we had decided to move to London. Overstrand Mansions, the flat I had found, was in an old Victorian block overlooking Battersea Park. Sean had a nice large room looking onto the park; with his desk under the window again, it was as near as was possible to the pattern of his Dublin room.

Sean had hoped, as the production of *Within the Gates* in America was such a success, and so well done, that it might have a major production in London. Michel Saint-Denis had suggested doing it at the Old Vic, but none of this happened. Shaw wrote to him about this in May of 1936.

There is no reason on earth why W.I.G. should not go on at the Old Vic if Lilian Baylis wants it. But as she has a competent producer (Guthrie) on her staff, there is equally no reason why you impose St. D. on her unless his qualifications are extraordinary and indispensible. An author can pick and choose his cast and even his staff for a West End production at a theatre hired ad hoc; but repertory theatres must be taken as they are, lock, stock (especially stock), and barrel. As to rehearsing, all an author can do is to produce the original performance so as to establish a tradition as far as possible; but beyond that he cannot go without ruining himself.

We are still in arrears and confusion after our 11 weeks at sea, and very old at that, Heaven help us; but we shall get straight presently and see something of you twain.

Earlier on when we lived in Chalfont St. Giles, we were desperately hard up. We were selling the amateur rights of Sean's first three plays to Samuel French for just £300 and 50 percent of the royalties and we needed some money in the interim. Sean asked G.B.S. for a loan.

G.B.S. sent him a cheque for £50 which was not in any way enough to settle our debts at the time. However once Sean had the royalties from the production of *Within the Gates* in America he was able to settle his debt with Shaw.

He received the following reply along with a copy of the cheque:

My dear Sean,

This is an improvident, extravagant and entirely unnecessary proceeding, most inconsiderate to your wife and children.

However, as I am powerless in the matter I beg to acknowledge receipt of your cheque for fifty pounds (50) sterling alleged to be due to me.

Swank, I call it.

G. Bernard Shaw

In Battersea, G.B.S. and Charlotte did not visit us in the flat we had taken. It was an old-fashioned block with no lifts, and we were on the fifth floor which was much too much of a climb for them. G.B.S. was now eighty.

So we started once more to visit with the Shaws. Sean and G.B.S. had many telephone conversations. Listening to the competition of two great Irishmen, outdoing each other in wit and sarcasm, was wonderful. They were generally very long conversations with much laughter.

Breon was about seven years old and Niall about two months, when on a visit to the Shaws, the conversation turned to schools. G.B.S. asked about Breon's school. Breon had gone to a small Quaker school in Chalfont St. Giles but we were looking for a school to send him to in London. Shaw amazed me a little by saying he had invested money in a school in Wimbledon. I knew by one of his prefaces in the play *Overruled* that he had a very advanced outlook on children, but I was surprised when he told me about the school in Wimbledon, called the Beltane School. I visited the school which I found to be a wonderful free type of education which I liked. This is where I sent Breon while we lived in Battersea. So it seemed that Shaw and I definitely thought the same on education.

Sean at this time was writing articles regularly for *Time and Tide*, a magazine that was run by Lady Rhonda. Lady Rhonda gave a luncheon for all the contributors of the magazine in their honour. At that time the contributors were people like Winifred Holtby and Vera Britten, etc. Sean, as a general contributor, was asked to the luncheon, with myself.

G.B.S. was also at the luncheon. He came over to me and said, "Now I have a chance to look after you, and have you to myself. Sean will be busy being questioned and interviewed." He was very gay and attentive, never leaving my side. G.B.S. sat at the head of one table and I sat on his right. A very austere lady sat next to me. She was very cross, more than cross, *furious* with me for getting so much attention from Shaw. Having asked me, was I Mrs. Sean O'Casey, she asked me what I did. I told her I was an actress, and worked for C. B. Cochran. She gave a sort of sniff, saying in a few words how often men of great intelligence tended to marry good-looking girls with not much intelligence. G.B.S. laughed and said he thought that Sean had shown great wisdom in marrying me. She then got more ruffled than ever—G.B.S. was looking at me with a twinkle in his eye, and I was playing up to him because she made me want to be more and more flippant! It was a good party—I enjoyed it.

Sean was writing a play called *The Star Turns Red*. At the same time, articles he had written for *Time and Tide*, on controversial issues, politics, theatre, etc., were collected together in a volume called *The Flying Wasp*. He had also started on his autobiography called *I Knock at the Door*.

In November of 1937, Sean wrote to G.B.S.

49 Overstrand Mansions
24 November 1937

My dear G.B.S.

I hope you are well. I've heard that Mrs. Shaw has been poorly, & I send, through you, my true sympathy. I'm just beginning to read (having read the preface) your *Immaturity*, lent to me, by the way, by a hard nut of an Irish Communist who was for a long time assistant to Jim Larkin in Dublin, & who is now here busy with the development of milk bars! *Immaturity* is the one novel of yours I've never read—never even heard of it, till my friend brought it along. I read all the others, bought second hand years & years ago in Dublin. It amused me to read of your Irish shyness, & ceased to amuse me when I realised that this very shyness & pride is deeply set in my own nature. However, it's better, thank God, than the frightful hypocrisy & maddening complacency of the English. No wonder Swift went mad. I was struck with the idea that a Communist is born a Communist, and (if he be not aware of it) is tormented till he discovers himself, or God's grace shows him his inborn nature. I am born Communist (as well as being practically born into Communism), for often as I have filled with anger at what Labour Leaders did & did not do; I have always come back to the belief that the workers alone have the words of eternal life.

I am just considering an offer from America of a house & garden, a car, and all arrangements made for me for the Education (I and Eileen have our own views on Education) of our two boys; and though I have great faith in the youth and vitality of the people of America, I'm afraid I'm a little too far spent to make a new life for myself & my family outside of this poor, timid, half-dead country—with a keen eye on the possibility of Ireland. A year or so ago I got an offer to help with the Theatre in Dartington Hall, but the offer seemed to stand in the way of free expression (I was to be very limited in my choice of work), so I reluctantly gave the back of my hand to it. Any way, I won't decide on anything till I finish, for good or ill, the writing of *The Star Turns Red*. I thought some time ago of writing something around the rebellion of Jack Cade. I was reading Froissart's Chronicles, & it interested me very much. What about you? You could make a Communist St. Joan of him.

All here (except myself, who have a cold) are well. The two boys, Breon & Niall growing into big intelligent Irishmen—each heavier & bigger than the scheduled size for their ages.

My love to you & Mrs. Shaw.

Sean

P.S. Don't bother to reply—just wanted to keep in touch with you both.

G.B.S. telephoned one day to say that he had been down to Totnes in Devon to visit the Elmhirsts at Dartington Hall. Dorothy and Leonard Elmhirst had a lovely estate stretching for many miles. On the estate was a very advanced modern school. G.B.S. was very enthusiastic about it and wanted us to lunch with him and Charlotte to discuss the school. Again, this great interest in our children's education. He said it had fine music and art facilities.

I had visited many modern coeducational schools wondering where to send Niall and Breon, but they were all very expensive and I had not found one that I liked entirely. When we did meet for lunch, Shaw insisted that Dartington Hall was the one school for the O'Casey children to go to. I said, "But how in the name of goodness are we possibly going to pay for it?" It was obviously a very expensive school. "Well," said G.B.S., waving his hand, "the money will come from somewhere, Eileen!" That is exactly where the money did come from—somewhere! God knows where.

Sean and I went down to visit Dartington Hall. It was very beautiful; lovely grounds and altogether it was very well equipped. We definitely liked it. But it was a difficult proposition because we did not want to board our children. I did not believe in boarding schools! I suppose, having been at one from the age of four, I felt I had good reason for this.

Back in Battersea we faced our problem. We decided we really loved the school, its atmosphere, lovely country surroundings, and excellent facilities for art, music, and theatre. So, we decided that we had to leave the flat and move to Totnes in Devon! After storing our furniture in London, we moved to Devon, and Breon went to the middle school immediately. Niall was then only two years old.

The Elmhirsts had arranged for us to stay at the Gate Lodge with the gardener and his wife; really quite a large lodge (we had two bedrooms and a sitting room), while we looked for a house.

We found a very large old Victorian house (we seemed to go in for Victorian dwellings); a conservatory on the left when entering the front door, a large garden in front, a small orchard outside the back door, a very large garage (which in the old days was for a carriage), stables at the back, and a large loft above. All were in a rather semi-dilapidated condition, but there was lots of space and a very low rent!

Our landlord was called Mr. Hawkins; he was a dentist. When he heard my husband was a playwright, he was very bothered, nearly beside himself, demanding he must have a guarantee and a reference. So Sean wrote to his friend G.B.S. for a guarantee of the rent and a reference. Shaw sent a long and amusing letter. I wonder we ever got the house.

17 October 1938

My dear Sean

Your landlord, being a dentist, has developed an extraction complex. He proposed a lease in which I was not only to guarantee all your covenants, but indemnify him for all the consequences. I said I did not know his character, but knew enough of yours to know that the consequences might include anything from murder to a European war; so I redrafted the agreement. The lawyers, knowing that their man was only too lucky to get a gilt-edged (as they thought) security, and that his demands were absurd, made no resistance. I mention it as you had better watch your step, not to say his, with the gentleman. Anyhow I had a bit of fun with him.

I seem to have picked up completely. The anaemia was not really pernicious.

I am glad to learn that the two miniature O'Caseys are happy among the young criminals at Dartington, and that their mother is now one of the Beauties of Devon.

Charlotte sends all sorts of affectionate messages.

G.B.S.

So here I was, stuck in Totnes, in the middle of the country, away from dear London, simply following G.B.S.'s wonderful advice! I knew I was going to miss London and our visits to G.B.S. Sean and I had always looked forward to the luncheons and meetings. Yes, I felt sad about this. Shaw meant a great deal to me, and this feeling was strengthened by his generous liking of

Sean's work. I find it hard to describe the hold Shaw's friendship had on me, but when I met him I felt completely at ease.

G.B.S. and Sean signed the lease of this house; whoever was our solicitor at the time must have it. I do know he was a relation of Napier Tandy. Sean's and G.B.S.'s signatures must be interesting to read on the lease.

When Sean settled in, he wrote to Charlotte Shaw saying that moving to Devon would be good for the children and that this is what mattered.

September 1938

Dear Mrs Shaw,

Thank you for the kindness you showed to us yesterday. The trek from here to Devon will, I'm sure, be a good thing for the two youngsters—and that matters most.

I have been searching my conscience, since you spoke to me, about my tendency towards quarrelling; but I don't think this tendency goes down deep in me. In all productions of my plays, I have had but one quarrel (with Norman Mac-Dermott), and that's saying a lot. The "quarrel" with the dentist landlord was just a flash rejecting the idea of "references." I can, and did, ask for a financial guarantee; but I'm not going to ask anyone to guarantee my morals. I can't say myself what sort I'll be a week from now. To be asked to get a moral guarantee from others, or one from myself, is, to me, stupid, and makes me mad. A long time ago I was asked to declare that a worker looking for the job of care-taker, was sober, honest, truthful, reliable, and industrious. I replied saying that what was wanted was a saint, and not a worker. And the man got the job!

I think my *Flying Wasp* did a little good. Recently, [James] Agate spoke at Toynbee Hall in favour of Government support of Music and Drama. Anyway, the book was just a continuation of what I said at a dinner given by the Critic's Circle

Sean O'Casey taken in Devon in the early 1950s.

(PHOTO BY WOLFGANG SUSCHITZKY)

in 1926, when I, foolishly, I suppose, told them my mind. They haven't asked me since.

I have always had to fight like the devil for life; but you must blame your husband, G.B.S., for whatever sharpness and wit that have come into my fighting qualities; and my young Dublin comrade, member of the fourth Order of St Francis, who first put the green-covered copy of *John Bull's Other Island* into my then reluctant hand. I am a fighter, to be sure. But, then Peter wasn't so great not lovable as his Master; but he was a forcible fellow and I am a forcible fellow, too.

> With many thanks and affectionate regards.
>
> Yours Sincerely,
>
> Sean O'Casey

I still did not feel that Charlotte understood Sean. Somehow she always seemed to rub him up the wrong way. She was always determined to have her own way and Sean also loved his own way—both hated to give in. She certainly had a fondness for Sean, but she still wanted to make him more tactful and not so outspoken. In other words, change his entire character.

CHAPTER
9

TINGRITH WAS the name of the house we had rented. It was on the main road from Totnes to Plymouth. Moving was a panic. When the furniture van arrived and the men started to unpack our belongings, Sean was running around like crazy wanting us to get his room ready. He had the most aggravating characteristic: An utterly compulsive desire to write would take him on Christmas Day, bank holidays, or other special days, but above all, whenever we moved house! So all the furniture men worked very much like in a Charlie Chaplin movie, at great speed, to get this one room finished. "Don't touch my books . . . Don't touch that . . . Can't you get rid of that old man?" —he'd say to me! ". . . My poor typewriter . . .," etc.

When he was settled into the room, it didn't matter that the rest of the house was in complete chaos, he was quite happy and settled down to his work. He was writing his second autobiography, *Pictures in the Hallway*.

Soon after we got to Totnes, war was being talked about, and eventually it happened—3rd September 1939! Now my life was taken up looking after evacuee children, helping with the war effort, and running concerts. It would take an entire book to describe all the happenings during the war, which lasted for six years!

After war was declared in Europe, speculation was mounting as to whether America would be drawn into the conflict. Shaw's postcard to Sean (10 October 1939) shows his political shrewdness over the development of the war:

> Don't bother about the U.S. They have it at full length in the Hearst papers. What the U.S. funked will, I hope, be in *The Manchester Guardian* tomorrow (Wednesday).
>
> G.B.S.

(The Hearst papers, some 20 dailies and a dozen Sunday newspapers owned by the powerful American magnate William Randolph Hearst, specialized in sensationalistic journalism, featuring big headlines and stories that strained the limits of credibility. They were known as the yellow press.)

When we had settled in Totnes, apart from his autobiography *Pictures in the Hallway*, Sean started his play, *Red Roses for Me*. Totnes had a market every Friday. Produce from all the farms around was auctioned—butter, cream, eggs, chickens, etc. Regularly, at this market was an old man who was there not to buy, but just to wander around. He buttonholed Sean—he was in a constant worry about his money at the bank. Was the bank to be trusted? I noticed all the time he was speaking to Sean, Sean was taking notes. He told me, "I'm putting him in my play, Eileen; he's a wonderful character." That is how Brennan o' the Moor came to life in *Red Roses for Me*.

Although we were living in Totnes, in Devon, and G.B.S. was in Ayot St. Lawrence, a distance of over two hundred miles, letters did pass between Sean and G.B.S.—some of which were lost.

How we missed him! When Shivaun was born in 1939 (September 28th), G.B.S. wrote a letter to me saying that sisterless men were always afraid of women. He also sent a checque for Shivaun.

4th Oct. 1939

My dear Eileen,

It is important that the boys should have a sister. Sisterless men are always afraid of women.

I enclose a birthday present for her. The next one will be only half a crown. The budget—oh, the Budget! The end of the year will clean me out.

We take it that you are doing as well as can be expected.

G. Bernard Shaw

At another time, Shaw wrote to Breon enclosing a packet of cards, with Shaw's photograph on them, signed, and told Breon that these could be sold to give him some pocket money. Some people thought that this was Shaw's conceit, but I found it very comical—a lovely thought!

Charlotte and G.B.S., then eighty-five years old, were in Ayot St. Lawrence during the war while Sean, fifty-nine years old, had a very active life with a young family. Every night there was bombing at Plymouth, and American soldiers billeted in Totnes visited him each day. Many were young men who had read his plays. We were also visited by some British soldiers billeted in Dartington. In spite of the distance and the demands made by the war, it seemed as if Shaw was very much a part of our lives. Sean was kept busy with his writings.

In February of 1940, *The Star Turns Red* was published, and later in the year the play was produced at the Unity Theatre in London. Sean was completing *Purple Dust*, and that play was published in November of 1940 (dedicated to Shivaun). Shaw wrote to Sean at this time, and asked him did he have a play for the Malvern Festival.

22 April 1940

Never heard of Mayokowski.

All well here.

I haven't been in a theatre for years; and I can't think of a new play, though the continuance of the Malvern Festival depends on my producing one. Can you oblige?

I should have gone to *The Red Star*, black-out if I hadn't read it. It showed up the illiteracy of the critics, who didn't know that like a good Protestant you had brought the language of the Authorized Version back to life.

Splendid!

G.B.S.

Sean replied a few days later:

Devon
29 April 1940

My dear G.B.S.

Fine to hear that all's well in Ayot St. Lawrence.

I've no play for Malvern. *Purple Dust* has been taken by Eddie Dowling of New York; & he'll be getting an option on the English License. He is very much struck with the play; & has, I believe, a part in it for himself. Dowling's father & mother were Irish, & he is Irish too! We're all Irish. Mr. Elmhirst was telling me he had lunch with you lately. They're doing part of your Film here. Good luck. Don't worry about Malvern & their mania for new plays. Haven't they hundreds to choose from. And a lot of yours, too.

God be wi' you,

Sean

Through the years, and throughout the war, Shaw kept in touch with us. In 1942 he wrote a postcard to Sean referring to Jacob Epstein's bust of Lady Gregory, for Sean had written to G.B.S. about his search for a photograph for his autobiography.

15/3/1942

The Epstein bust was a failure because E. changed his plan when he was half-way through and ended with a muddle of the two. Besides, he was always seeking to reveal the aboriginal savage beneath the civilized sitter; and nothing could change Augusta into a Brooklyn washerwoman, much less into a half humanized lizard.

If I can find the negatives I shall try to get some better prints for you.

G.B.S.

At the end of 1942, Sean and Shaw wrote letters to each other about Breon—and about Charlotte.

14th November 1942

My dear Sean,

Don't on your life bring up your boy as that most despicable of all shams, a stage Irishman. A man's country is the one whose air he breathes and whose people he knows. Breon is an Englishman, born in British Battersea, bred in British Devon, singing Drake's Drum and not Let Erin Remember; having Raleigh for his local hero. To him his dad must always be a funny sort of fellow, let us hope beloved and admired, but still a curiosity. O'Flaherty, whom he calls O'Flayerty, is a native of a savage island, who seems to take it as a matter of course that his mother should be a thief and a liar who, by way of being patriotic, claims that all great Englishmen were Irish. Like Queen Victoria, he is "not amused." Why should he be? And aren't you glad he isn't?

· 107 ·

Why do you add "strangely enough"? The air has made an honest English lad of him; that is all. Sixty-six years of English air have not made an Englishman of me because I started with 20 years of Irish air. Battersea and Devon have by this time marked Breon for their own; and nothing could be more wicked than to rob him of his birthright.

By the way, he will be greatly hampered by his father's fame if he does not change his name. Think of Mozart's son! of Wagner's son! of that unlucky Mendelsohn who said "I have been the son of my famous father and the father of my famous son, but never myself." If he intends to become famous he had better call himself O.K.C. Totneson or Devonson.

Charlotte is an invalid now; and we are both damnably old.

Pearson's book is all right as to the facts, and very readable. I helped him all I could.

That's all for today. I am sorry I wasn't in London when your consort came up. It is pleasanter to see her than it is to see me in my decrepitude.

G.B.S.

I remember once when I wrote to G.B.S. from London, asking him if I could go down to Ayot St. Lawrence to visit Charlotte, the answer was "No." He told me that Charlotte was disfigured by her illness and would not really like me to see her, and also she was very ill. This was a long and interesting letter, which I received while staying in London with some friends, and I regret very much it was lost.

G.B.S. was utterly devoted to Charlotte and during her illness had moved the piano into the hall so that she could hear him playing in the distance from her room. G.B.S. was a very fine pianist.

Bust of George Bernard Shaw by Auguste Rodin.

(PHOTO BY WOLFGANG SUSCHITZKY)

In September of 1943, Shaw wrote to Sean to tell him of Charlotte's death.

29/9/1943

We came up to London, after an absence that ran into years, on the 26th of July, my birthday (87); and Charlotte's death on the 12th of this month involves a heap of business that will keep me here for weeks to come.

The spate of letters, 80 a day for a fortnight, was over whelming; I had to acknowledge them in the lump by a notice in *The Times*, but still there were several that had to be answered.

The end was to be expected at our ages (86 and 87). It was quite happy; and I was tempted to put into the notice "No letters; no congratulations."

A letter has just come from Cosgrave—along with yours! Very friendly.

G.B.S.

Two years later Sean wrote the following letter.

17th February 1945

Dear G.B.S.

I am about to bother you with a question—two as a matter of fact: Have you got in your library the following books— *Cambridge History of English Literature*, Volumes 4 and 5; and *History of English Literature* by Legouis?

Should you have them, could you lend them to me? Breon, our eldest, is preparing for some examination under the aegis of Dartington, and he has been called upon to memorise most of these books. They are in the Dartington Library, but there is such a call on them that they rarely can come into his hands. If you have them, and let me have them, I shall warn him to take great care of them, though unable to guarantee their return in perfect condition. He is a lad, however, who takes great care of books, and has still even the childish ones got for him when he was a kid.

If you haven't time—and I imagine, like myself, you haven't, having little use for them—don't bother your sage head about the inquiry, but forget it ever came.

I have just finished correcting proofs of the third vol. of semi-autobiography—*Drums Under the Windows*—which is to appear in the spring. And I've written a war play—*Oak Leaves and Lavender*; or *A World on Wallpaper* which Bronson Albery has taken for production when he can get a cast. Nathan says it's a fine play, far and away the best play on war he has encountered for years.

I am sending a cutting from *International Literature*—No. 3, 1944, showing reproduction of an engraving of yourself, which looks to be a fine one. And a cutting from *New York Times Book Review* showing a photograph of yourself which, I think, can't compare with the engraving. You have probably got both of them, but then you mightn't. And a cutting from *I.L.* giving a review of your *Pygmalion*. We are all well here, the children growing a pace, and staying healthy and strong. It is easier here now since the bombing stopped—it was a nuisance hurrying the children down to the Morrison Shelter in the middle of the night, particularly when your own mind wasn't feeling too steady at all. The workers seem to be coming into some of their own at last. This new International of Labour should be a force for good among men and women.

I do hope you are well and feeling fit. Recently, I had a bad chill which got into the chest and crept down to a lung, but I fought away, well out of it all, and am "all gay" again as the soldiers used to say.

I see we were together in the last number of *The Bell*. Eileen sends her love, and so do I.

Ever yours,

Sean

This bond between Sean and G.B.S. was part of our lives. I have felt latterly that they were like two old characters exchanging notes on their various complaints—Sean's eyes which were not at all good and G.B.S.'s "legs not so good."

Sean wanted permission to use two letters G.B.S. had written to him in his future volume of autobiography.

12 August 1945

My dear G.B.S.

Greetings. I hope you are well. All well here, except that I am under a periodic week or two trouble with my eyes. I am, however, well used to it, and so far, doesn't do much harm, bar the discomfort of the pain.

I want to ask your permission to use, in future work, your letter to me when I asked you for a preface to *Three Shouts on a Hill*, and, maybe, one or two of the others, including the letter you sent me commenting on the play called *The Silver Tassie*.

Breon has, apparently, got over the difficulty of getting suitable history books. The reason I asked was that he is a mortally shy fellow (mostly), as tall as you, now—six foot one. Looks as if the war would soon end, and that, at long last, we may have something to thank God for. By the way, I'm afraid De Valera's heart isn't so warm as you think it is. He was one who stopped poor schoolchildren from getting meals, because that would be "the thin edge of the wedge of Communism." All the best.

Ever yours,

Sean O'Casey

Shaw had written a letter to a Dr. Newman suggesting he send his book to Sean. The book was *Mind, Sex, and War*. Dr. Newman was a psychiatrist at Oxford City and Mental Hospital. Sean did not really think this a kind act, even if it was meant so!

Totnes, Devon
15 October 1945

Dear G.B.S.

Oh! why did you write such a kind, if bewildered, letter to Dr. Newman? He sent his book to me, accompanied by an explanatory letter in which he says that "the book must be read straight through and at one go." The tale of 250 visits to the one play, and a very bad play too. Since I got the book, he has rung me up twice. Eileen answered to say I was out, in the hope that he would understand that I was unwilling to say anything. But he is to ring up again and again I suppose till he forces me to tell him what I think of it.

Any man who would venture on a work like this ought to be psychiatrised himself—there must be something astray in him. He says "please keep the book, if only as a memento of the kindness of heart of G.B.S." Your kindness of heart has brought sin into the O'Casey fold, and a lot of woe.

Here's one sentence about the play written by G. J. Nathan: "They come pretty bad at times, these English imports . . . but they do not often come quite so entirely bad as this one." That's the play Newman went 250 times to see! God forgive him—and you.

My warmest regards,

Sean

The play in question was Rattigan's *Flarepath*, dedicated to Newman, which was staged in London during 1942 and ran for over six hundred performances.

Sean was getting periodicals from Ireland. He was particularly interested in *The Bell*, a very elite monthly literary magazine, and received a letter from its editor, Peadar O'Donnell, saying that he had written to Shaw but had never got an answer. Sean sent the following letter to G.B.S.

TC. O'Casey
Totnes, Devon
17 August 1948

Dear G.B.S.

Enclosed is a letter from a friend in Dublin. He was for a time the Editor of *The Bell*. He has asked me to write to you to see if you would write a preface to a book written by Tom Barry on what happened during the I.R.A.'s fight with the Black and Tans and Auxies. Barry was a Brigadier of an I.R.A. Cork Brigade. The writer of the letter to me—Peadar O'Donnell—complains, as you can see, that letters to you from him get no reply. I am writing to tell him that he isn't a bird alone. That you have more important things to do than answering letters; and, that, even if you do, you won't be likely to agree with his request.

I shouldn't forward this letter of his to you if it didn't appear that you seemed to be more interested in things Irish now than you used to be; and so I didn't like to withhold the letter to prevent you from being bothered.

Well, there it is: for you to answer, to ignore, or to write the preface, as you will.

All the best with our love.

Yours as ever,

Sean O'Casey

G.B.S. was offered the Freeman of the City of Dublin, and Sean wrote him this letter:

TC. O'Casey
Totnes, Devon
19 February 1946

Dear G.B.S.

Greetings and congratulations on becoming a Freeman of Dublin's fair city; Ptolemy's Eblana (or was it Strabo), the Danes' Dyflinnisk, and the Gaels' B'lah Cliath of the Golden Goblets.

Sooner or later, we'll see you in stone in one of the parks or erect in one of the streets—in stone or bronze.

What a pity about *Caesar and Cleopatra*. Apparently, too much money has spoiled it all. I'm sorry you didn't go in for *The Devil's Disciple* first. This play would have lent itself to a grand film production, I think. I remember mentioning it years ago, years and years ago, but Mrs Shaw didn't like the idea.

All the best to you.
Yours very sincerely,

Sean O'Casey

These letters between Sean and G.B.S. were very valuable to us during the period of the war, because it was the one way of cementing our friendship.

CHAPTER
❦ 10 ❧

AFTER THE war I used to go by train to London now and again for a few days, which meant I could go and see G.B.S. in his home at Ayot St. Lawrence.

There was no doubt he was very lonely after Charlotte's death. He travelled very little now he was alone, but he still had the urge to write, producing his last full length play, *Buoyant Billions,* which was to be his final production in London.

On one particular occasion, I was delighted to hear from John Dulanty, who was then the High Commissioner for Ireland in London. He had been to see Shaw on a business trip, and Shaw had suggested that it might be an opportunity for me to be taken from door to door. Shaw wrote:

12/1/50

Yes; come on Saturday at 3:30. Dulanty has a car, and knows the way from door to door, which is the only tolerable way of reaching this remote village.

If he does not come with you, there is nothing for it but

a taxi from Welwyn *Garden City* (not Welwyn) or a car hired from Kensington 5257 where there is a driver who knows the way.

The terminus for W.G.C. is King's Cross.

G.B.S.

I used to love these visits. G.B.S. always expressed his admiration, and how he looked forward to being with me. This is always very nice for any woman.

Following the visit, Dulanty wrote to Sean saying that G.B.S. greeted me with, "Well, Eileen, you have still got your good looks!" He went on to write: "He was extremely delighted to see her. I wandered out of the room to give them the opportunity of a mild flirtation."

Dulanty was a delightful person with an amazing sense of humour. Sean and he were great friends. Shaw must have been ninety-four years of age at the time.

Shaw used to dwell on his youth, reminiscing as most people do when they get old. He talked a great deal of his early days in Dublin. As a young boy his mother had a girl who helped in the house. Often Shaw was sent out for walks with the girl, but instead of going to the park or by the sea, she would take him to the pub where her boyfriends were drinking—or to visit her friends in the very poor districts of Dublin. Vividly he remembered the look of povery and all it meant, and the hatred of poverty was to remain with him forever.

His dislike of drink also developed at an early age. His father wasted a great deal of money on drink, and Shaw saw the misery it brought to his mother and the family. It made a lifelong impression on him. Sean also had a violent hatred of drink. His mother suffered greatly when his brother, Mick, who was many years older than Sean, used to come home drunk, screaming and yelling, upsetting his mother as he knocked the place to bits. G.B.S. was a teetotaller, and Sean was almost one.

Shaw insisted that when Sean was a boy, although very poor and suffering from malnutrition, he had freedom to play in the streets and rub shoulders with his neighbours, thereby having the chance to share their sorrows and their joys. Sean's life was hard, but full of love and laughter. G.B.S. came from the genteel poverty class, as I did, and we had a more restricted childhood.

During my school holidays my mother and I would live in "rooms," and I remember wanting to go and play with the landlady's children. I was not allowed to do this, as my mother insisted on "keeping ourselves to ourselves," and, in her view, it was not suitable for me to play with these children. This meant that I had rather a lonely existence as a child. My mother spent all the spare money on drink, and there was nothing left for my entertainment, and I hardly went out at all. Mine was the same sort of "genteel poverty" background as Shaw's, although I think he was better off than I was. Shaw came from the lower middle class, whereas Sean was brought up completely in the slums of Dublin.

Sean idolised his mother. Some of his best writing refers to her, also to Lady Gregory. It seemed to me that it was much easier for Sean to express his affection; Shaw, on the other hand, found it hard to express his feelings of love. Only in his love letters did he excel himself.

On one occasion I spoke to G.B.S. about Sean's play *Cock-A-Doodle Dandy,* the last play Sean had written. Shaw thought it was a magnificent play but doubted it would be a commercial success. He indicated that Sean should think of a play which might make money! I was furious over this remark and said so! He told me he and Charlotte had been to Lourdes and found it quite an impressive sight.

"Of course," I said, "I do not doubt it was a very impressive sight, but Sean is writing deeply about the superstition of it all. I quite agree it is not a money spinner of a subject, but there you are. After all, you yourself have written things showing up the doctors, or showing up regimentation, so why should not Sean write about what he wants to?"

Photograph of the O'Casey family
on George Bernard Shaw's desk at Shaw's Corner.

(PHOTO BY WOLFGANG SUSCHITZKY)

He laughed, offered me another cup of tea, and said that it was fun arguing with me, as I was such a champion of Sean's writing, and what a lucky man he was to have me!

Having noticed some cameras on a shelf, I said to him, "I know that you are proud of the fact that you are a first-class photographer."

He replied, "Indeed I am. Nobody will ever take a bad photograph of me. I know exactly how to stand, and the best angle of my face."

He talked of the films that had been made of his plays *Major Barbara* and *Pygmalion* and how much he had enjoyed the filming of them. His face lit up with excitement while he was telling me about this.

On another visit I had a photograph of the children with me. He was so utterly delighted to see Sean's family that he said he wanted a copy of his own. I gave him my copy and he kept it on the study table at Ayot St. Lawrence. His face lit up, and he laughed, saying again, "I really envy Sean. It is lovely to see such fine offspring." It seemed to me that he truly did envy Sean and the warmth of our family. This was the same photograph that I saw when I visited Shaw's house all those years later.

The hours seemed to pass unnoticed when we talked, and it was often dusk when I left him to return to London. His wit and humour were still very keen. He was rather unsteady on his legs, but his eyesight was good.

After this visit he wrote to Sean:

> Ayot St. Lawrence
> Welwyn, Herts.
> 6th May 1950

My dear Sean,

Eileen, still lovely as ever, gave me a photograph of the lot of you which pleased me so much that I have had it framed and look at it quite often. Your marriage has been a eugenic success; the Heir apparent is a stalwart who must

George Bernard Shaw's desk, Shaw's Corner.

(PHOTO BY WOLFGANG SUSCHITZKY)

count me as a Struldbrug, which is what I actually look like. I keep my wits about me much better than my legs; that is the best I can say for myself.

Ireland, no longer under Dublin Castle and Grand Jury Government, cannot now brood on her wrongs for cash from America and heroic and romantic sympathy from the rest of the world. In the old days we were the first flower of the earth and the first gem of the sea, our only rival being Poland, where hope for a season bade the world farewell, and freedom shrieked when Kosciusko fell. Now we are an insignificant cabbage garden in a little islet quite out of the headlines; and our Fianna Fail Party is now The Unionist Party and doesn't know it. I have nothing to tell them except that the Ulster capitalists will themselves abolish the Partition when the Labour Party is strong enough to threaten them with an Irish 1945 at the polls, and they must have the support of the Catholic agricultural south to avert it. But all they do is to send me medals of the Blessed Virgin, guaranteeing, if I say a novena, that she will give me anything I ask from her, to which I reply that the B.V. needs helpers and not beggars.

I have no news for you except the quite uninteresting item that I am having a bout of lumbago. They are trying to bake it out of me by Radiant Heat.

G. Bernard Shaw

Sean wrote in reply:

Totnes, Devon
1 August 1950

My very dear G.B.S.

In a way, I am glad circumstances prevented you from seeing my friend. I don't like the responsibility of sending friends down on other friends. There's a touch of "unfairity" in it. One who may be charming to me may well be a bore to another; and, besides, one can't get intimate with another in an acquaintance of an hour's duration. Tom Curtiss may try to see you when he returns from Paris in six or eight weeks time, in the forlorn hope that you may have found a maid by then. I have been washing up every day since the war started, and am well used to it now. A letter to me from Desmond McCarthy complains of "creators" having to do such work, and St. John Ervine recently complained of the same fact. But why shouldn't we all have to do some useful work, if we are fit for it? I hear our children often talking now of useful work—the seniors are painting the facade of the school; and each junior has to take his or her turn in the kitchen, carrying wood or serving at tables. Our boy, Niall, is quite a good cook; and the eldest, Breon, who is away in art-school in London, has to do for himself in this way—buy his food, and cook it, before he can eat it. We are all learning a little more about life. And not a bad thing either.

I am very pleased to know that the picture of the family hangs on your wall; and proud, too. It is a long time since I got from you the letter of sharp advice not to depend on Bernard Shaw's preface, but on what I wrote myself. Advice which made me curse for a few moments, but which I soon saw to be the one advice to take; and took it resolutely and carried it out; a fierce and fine resolution which brought the picture of myself and family to hang honorably on the wall of Ireland's greatest man. I won't bother you again about a friend. I have been often asked to ask you to see this person, that person. When I decline, they say, resentfully, I thought you were a friend of Bernard Shaw's and I bewilder some of them by saying That's why I won't bother him; if I were an enemy of his, I'd send you to him readily enough. I see our friend, John Dulanty will be soon leaving his post, outpost for Eirinn. Ireland has few Dulantys, and the chap to replace him will find it hard going to follow Dulanty, much more to keep up with him.

Take care of yourself, great care of yourself—there's no budding Bernard Shaw in Ireland. My deep love to you, and Eileen's too.

Yours most sincerely,

Sean

In the autumn of 1950, I heard that G.B.S. was ill, having fallen from an apple tree in his garden, which had resulted in his breaking his leg. He had to go to hospital and after the operation he developed pneumonia. He was unhappy in hospital, *very* unhappy, and could not wait to come out.

When G.B.S. returned home, Dulanty, then High Commissioner from Ireland, telephoned us in Devon, saying that G.B.S. wanted to see me, and could I go to him immediately. I could not get there soon enough. On arriving at the house in Ayot St. Lawrence I saw that one of the downstairs rooms had been turned into a bedroom for Shaw.

He was lying in a high hospital bed by the wall. Under the window, looking out onto the garden was a couch-bed onto which he could be lifted to lie for a few hours during the day.

It was a very orderly and austere room, very light. On the wall I did notice a picture of Stalin and a picture of Gandhi. G.B.S. looked very frail and ill.

He was a very fastidious and aesthetic man. Even at this stage, his mind was still very keen and laughingly he told me, in a very weak voice, how a Catholic nurse had had a go at converting him, but he found it tedious as well as funny.

I feel compelled to borrow a sentence from Eleonor O'Connor, who had nursed him in hospital. She told that Shaw had commented on his hospital stay: "They wash me all the time; they massage me; when I'm asleep they wake me; when I'm awake they ask me why I'm not asleep—routine, routine."

He smiled, and I held his hand—he had lovely hands.

*Photographs on wall
by George Bernard Shaw's bed.*
LEFT TO RIGHT: *Gandhi, General Djerjinski, Lenin, Stalin.*

(PHOTO BY WOLFGANG SUSCHITZKY)

I knew he would have loved to make his hundredth birthday, and I tried to persuade him that he might get better and yet see this birthday.

He was then ninety-four years old, but he clearly hated the idea of being helped from his bed to the couch. In fact he hated being obliged to depend on others. He really wanted to die. He asked about Sean and the children.

He also asked how Sean was financially. I could not possibly have answered other than I did; that of course we were perfectly all right. He said he had heard we were in clover (which we most certainly were not) and that he was very relieved.

He talked of his loneliness and the death of so many of his contemporaries and friends. He spoke of all this in his lovely Irish voice. He was extremely tired, so when he closed his eyes I crept from the room quietly.

I wrote a letter describing this visit in which I said to Sean:

I was so grateful you have us, darling, when I saw Shaw so alone, even with his comfort and attendance.

He is in a very plain orderly room, I suppose his bedroom, on a sort of raised bed. He has flannel sheets, and the room is very warm. He has pictures of Stalin, Gandhi, and I could not quite make out the General, and himself. He is a great person; so are you, dearest. I am so glad you have me, bad and all as I am, and the children.

Shaw said to me "I'm finished now. It's up to Sean" and said "my love to all the O'Caseys."

A few days later I had a desperate urge to go to Ayot St. Lawrence again. I could not stop thinking of Shaw.

I called Dulanty's office in London. Dulanty told me he had just telephoned Sean in Devon to ask where I could be found. G.B.S. said he wanted to see me again. I rang his house at once, and they told me to come, if possible, that afternoon.

On arrival I found G.B.S. dozing. He looked pale and ill, so very frail. Finally, he opened his eyes, and turning to me he said: "I really think I am going to die."

His voice was very weak. He spoke so softly that I had to get close to him to hear what he was saying. He rallied for a moment and began to talk, saying he wondered what was going to happen after death, and who he was going to meet.

"If there is an Almighty, Eileen, I'll have a hell of a lot of questions to ask Him!"

He slipped back to sleep again, first asking me not to go yet. Though so frail and sick, his brain was as clear and as bright as ever. I stole from the room, believing I ought to go. I was talking to the nurse when the bell rang from his room. He asked if I had gone, because he wanted to say goodbye. Though a little reluctant, the nurse whispered to me, "If you are not too long with him this time—he is very anxious to see you."

On my return he gave me one of his lovely smiles. He said his head was aching always, and he asked me to stroke his forehead. I spoke to him gently.

"It is wonderful to have the softness of a woman's hand, and a gentle voice."

I stroked his forehead until he was sleepy.

"Kiss me goodbye," he asked. I kissed him, and then noticed that a trace of my lipstick had remained on his lips. I gently wiped it away with my handkerchief, and there was this wicked twinkle in his eye which I had always loved.

"Goodbye and God bless you," I whispered.

"He has blessed you already," he answered.

He sank back into sleep, and I left, knowing that I would never see him again.

Two days later the expected news of his death came. I had lost someone I had dearly loved, and Sean had lost probably his best friend; the man who stood by him and defended him always.

The words "He has blessed you already" ring in my mind to this day.

G.B.S. at Coole Park, April 1915.

(PHOTO BY W. F. BAILEY; COLLECTION OF COLIN SMYTHE)

APOLLO THEATRE

Phone Gerrard 6970} 6971} Shaftesbury Avenue. W.1.

PROPRIETORS	APOLLO THEATRE CO., LTD.
CHAIRMAN	LEE SHUBERT

EVENINGS AT 8.15
MATINEES: THURSDAY and SATURDAY at 2.30

By arrangement with ROBERT LORAINE

CHARLES B.

COCHRAN'S PRODUCTION

"THE SILVER TASSIE"

A Tragi-Comedy
by
SEAN O'CASEY

Characters in the order of their appearance:

Sylvester Heegan	BARRY FITZGERALD
Simon Norton	SIDNEY MORGAN
Mrs. Heegan	EITHNE MAGEE
Susie Monican	BEATRIX LEHMANN
Mrs. Foran	UNA O'CONNOR
Teddy Foran	IAN HUNTER
Harry Heegan	CHARLES LAUGHTON
Jessie Taite	BILLY BARNES
Barney Bagnal	S. J. WARMINGTON
The Croucher	LEONARD SHEPHERD
1st Soldier	CHARLES LAUGHTON
2nd Soldier	IAN HUNTER
3rd Soldier	BARRY FITZGERALD
4th Soldier	JACK MAYNE
5th Soldier	G. ADRIAN BYRNE
6th Soldier	S. J. WARMINGTON
The Corporal	SINCLAIR COTTER
The Visitor	IVO DAWSON
The Staff Wallah	ALBAN BLAKELOCK
The Trumpeter	EMLYN WILLIAMS
1st Stretcher Bearer	NORMAN STUART
2nd Stretcher Bearer	OSWALD LINGARD
3rd Stretcher Bearer	CHARLES SCHOFIELD
4th Stretcher Bearer	BARRY BARNES
1st Casualty	CLIVE MORTON
2nd Casualty	JAMES WILLOUGHBY
Surgeon Forby Maxwell	HASTINGS LYNN
The Sister of the Ward	AUDREY O'FLYNN

Staged under the direction of RAYMOND MASSEY

Oct. 11

The cast of the original production of *The Silver Tassie*, opening night
October 11, 1929.

APPENDIX

St. John Ervine's letter to Ron Ayling of September 12th, 1957.

Dear Mr. Ayling,

The only reason I haven't included O'Casey as one of G.B.S.'s friends, is that he wasn't. You can do a man a kindness, and G.B.S. was incessant in kindness, without being his intimate. It will surprise me to hear that Sean was ever in G.B.S.'s house, except, perhaps, once or twice to lunch. I certainly never saw him there, and I'm sure that if O'Casey had ever gone to Whitehall Court during the eighteen months that G.B.S. and I were neighbours there, he'd have had me in to keep him company with Sean. He nearly always did that, because, he said, I had the gift of the gab, and could keep the conversation going, which he was not always able to do. No one can possibly believe that O'Casey was a friend of G.B.S. in the same way that William Archer was. It was charming to see Archer and G.B.S. together. I remember once, in a theatre, seeing them together through the chance that their seats adjoined. Mine was immediately in front of theirs. A blind, deaf, dumb and deeply stupid man could have seen that these two were old and affectionate friends, who had no need to display their feeling because it was transparent. G.B.S. was an affectionate man as well as a very kind and generous one, and he clung to his old friends very closely. Merely to go for a walk with Archer was meat and drink to him. The war, which knocked my right leg off, put paid to my walking account with him, but, luckily, he had a great affection for my wife and she not only took *her* walks with him, but took mine, too; and he talked to her in the easy way he had with people he liked, and about everything from God to Sidney Webb. (My typing is terrible today, but I'm the world's champion ass with machinery. I can't do anything with it, but mess it up.) G.B.S. was a good companion to those he liked and knew well, but he was incredibly shy with mere acquaintances and strangers, and I've seen him blush with embarrassment on entering a room which he had expected to be unoccupied, and finding strangers there.

No, I don't agree with you in the least that my failure to record O'Casey's relations with him is at fault in the book. How could I have recorded it. It never existed as an important fact. You are not a man's bosom pal because you do him a good turn. G.B.S. never had any cause to do Sidney Webb a good turn, but no one who knew them failed to perceive what good friends they were, a fact which is all the more remarkable because G.B.S. did not like Beatrice—who could like her, that walking automatic machine?—and she did not like him. You should have seen G.B.S. with people like Granville Barker and Gilbert Murray. He overflowed with good spirits when he was in the company he enjoyed, but he was silent as the grave in that of strangers or uncongenial people.

I have always said that G.B.S. would do more for his friends than they would do for themselves.

Yours sincerely,

St. John Ervine

Letter from Sean O'Casey to Ron Ayling.

Devon.

3 November, 1957

Ron Ayling, Esq.

Dear Ron,

Well, well! I've read with interest the extracts from the letters sent to you by St. John Ervine and Austen Clarke. Austen C. camouflages the events of 1926 very nicely; but hardly hides them all. "By collecting uncomplimentary references"; and why not? They are often more interesting than the opposites; but I fear, they went farther than being just "uncomplimentary." The "exploitation of the poorer class" to me was a slander. I never said there was a "cabal" against me in Dublin. The outburst of opposition was probably spontaneous, but I did say in my autobiography that there was a cabal against Yeats. I know, because I was asked to join it. Whether Clarke had anything to do with it or no, I'm not sure. My own belief is that he hadn't, that he would be above it. O'Flaherty was the core of it, for he disliked Yeats for some reason. A.C. couldn't have read my biographical books when he ventures to say I never faced the fact that the biggest injury I suffered was the rejection of the *S. Tassie*. I think I faced the fact, faced Yeats, L. Gregory and L. Robinson pretty firmly; though it would have been better—materially—for me to have been humble, and kept my mouth shut. This is the first time I have heard that A.E. had been "running O'C as a sort of political

St. John Ervine, British novelist,
dramatist, and critic, 1922.

(HULTON PICTURE CO.)

propaganda for some time." Isn't it obvious, too, then, 1926, I should have been a damn bad propaganda weapon for A.E.—even were I willing to become one—seeing then that I was rather infamous than famous? As for "Nationalism," his anxiety to defend it amuses me. I was never aware that either he or F.R.H. did much for it; I never heard of them in the Gaelic League, the Republican Movement, or saw them on a hurling field, the time I was half killing myself for them all, organising Camogie Clubs, secretary of a hurling club, secretary of a Pipers Band, teaching Irish four nights a week, speaking on platforms and doing a damn hard days work before tackling any of them. Now he comes along to hint or say that I was predjucing [sic] the nationalism of the country. He isn't quite frank when he says that he never tried to assess the ultimate value of my plays. He has forgotten the long review he had in the *Irish Times* of *Cock-A-Doodle Dandy,* the most peculiar and bittersweet review I have ever received of that play. I quoted a poem of his in *The Green Crow,* referring to him as being no mean poet, and a man of no mean mind which he probably hasn't read. In Dublin, he mentioned this to my daughter, saying he had heard I had said something kind about him in the book. But I don't want to think any harm of Austen. He has had a damn hard time of it, and doesn't make much from his work. I wrote to America about him, trying to get some attention for him there, and I wish I could help him more effectively. But he lacks the aggressive spirit, that of the fighter, so essential if one believes one has a mission, be it politics, poetry, painting or playwrighting. I wish he were a bolder spirit; for he has been brave in clinging to his poetry against many odds, and he is a very good reviewer of other poets' work. Indeed, I have a cautious affection for Austen. A Catholic in Ireland, if he has any thought, has a bad time of it. I think he is a proud fellow in his own way, and I admire him for that same. I wonder how or where St. John Ervine got his dogmatism?

He is more dogmatic on everything under the sun than a newly-fledged Irish Bishop. I have no doubt that G.B.S. was a friend of his and of W. Archer, but, I imagine, in a limited way. I imagine that it was St.J. who walked with Shaw rather than it was Shaw who walked with St.J. Mrs. St.J. was a friend of Mrs. Shaw rather than of G.B.S. I imagine it was Mrs. St.J. who talked of God to Shaw rather than vice versa, possibly in an effort to win Shaw from his unbelief, as so many tried to do, the last, an Irish nurse when Shaw was in hospital with his broken thigh. I don't know what St.J. means by "You can do a man a kindness, and Shaw was incessant in kindness, without being his intimate." What is he hinting at here? If he means that I was personally beholden to Shaw, or that I received from him any of this incessant kindness, then, plainly speaking, St. John Ervine is a liar. As a matter of fact, St.J. wouldn't have understood, and can't now the bond between me and G.B.S. Here are a few: He was a Dublinman, so was I; he was reared up a Protestant, so was I; he suffered from living in the genteel poverty of the Irish lower middle-class while I suffered the squalid, but more vigorous poverty of the proletariat; Shaw was mainly a self-educated man, so was I; Shaw hated poverty in all its forms, so did I; Shaw fought against it most of his life, so did I, and still do; Shaw thought Stalin a great man, so did I, and so do still; Shaw was passionately devoted to the USSR, and all the USSR did and was doing, so was I; Shaw hated all British Imperialism, so did I; Shaw rejected the Christian beliefs, so did I; Shaw saw through the romantic idea of Irish Nationalism, so did I; Shaw was a fighter, and he knew I was one, too (I've never heard that he ever said in a letter to St.J. "Bravo, Titan!"); in almost his last words to Mrs. O'C he said, "It is for Sean, now, to carry on the fight"; Not St.J. but Sean; Shaw was a born Communist, so was I; Shaw called Jim Larkin "the greatest Irishman since Parnell," and Shaw knew how I had fought for the workers with Jim; Shaw was deeply interested in the

Chinese Workers' and Peasants Red Army and its long and terrible march from Kiangsi in the south to Shensi in the north, wondering if they could do it, and if they did, what effect it would have on the whole of China, so was I; though I'm sure St.J. never even heard of it until the Red Army eventually broke through in Manchuria, and, finally, won China for Communism; Shaw had a deep affection for Lady Gregory, so had I (I hope St.J. won't next say somewhere I was never a friend of hers; but he'd hardly do that, for he disliked her, I imagine, or, certainly, she did him); his initials are carved on the great tree in Coole, so are mine, but I've never seen St.J's there; while St.J. mentions a number of American Drama Critics, I notice he never mentions Nathan, yet Nathan had a deep reverence for Shaw, and Shaw thought highly of him, and so did, do, I; although his name is not mentioned either, Shaw was always delighted to see John Dulanty, the then High Commissioner for Ireland—it was he who brought the Roll of Dublin's Freeman to G.B.S.; Shaw loved his humor and his stories, and so did I; Shaw was always ready to talk about Ireland, and so was I.

Well, there are a few of the affinities that went to and fro between Shaw and me, cutting out, even, the tremendous interest we both took in the Theater; affinities that could hardly have existed between St.J. and the Dublin sage. Again, if Mrs. St.J. was so dear to G.B.S, why didn't he ask to see her during his last days? He asked for Eileen, not once, but several times; and it was she who was with him just before he sank into his last long sleep. Why didn't he give his last message to St.J? On the 22 Oct. a letter from a Dublin friend (now in a London job), Seumas Scully, 20 Mountview Road, Stroud Green, London, N.4., says "Have been to Shaw's house, and saw your family photo there on the mantlepiece." How did that come there—will St.J. tell us? Perhaps he knows that O'Casey stole into the house on a dark night and placed it there. It is also odd that St.Jay never mentions—if I remember right—Shaw's friendship for Lady Gregory, though he was very fond of her. Why? Shaw's name is carved on the Coole tree, and I have a photograph of G.B.S. sitting on the border of Coole Lake (sent to me by Shaw himself), with one of the Old Lady, and one of Yeats in his younger days (very handsome) standing before the background of Coole Park trees. Why wasn't she admitted to Shaw's friendship by St. Jay? I imagine because he disliked the Old Lady, and so shoved her out, as far as he could, from Shaw's circle.

When I first came to London, I never sought out Shaw; it never entered my mind to do so; I never even thought of him much, never at all in the way of a visit, for it never dawned on me that he would be interested in any way with me or my work—very little at that time. I have never bothered to mingle with the famous; rather am I interested in the folk. When I was at Cambridge, I sought out, not the dons (though many of them have great minds and great souls), but the students. I hadn't an idea even where Shaw lived, and I was very surprised to get an invitation to lunch, not to Whitehall Court, but to Adelphi Terrace. It may surprise St.Jay to hear that I went to Adelphi Terrace several times. Only once was Shaw and his wife invited by us, and by Eileen who thought we should ask them to us after so many visits to them. We couldn't afford lunches and dinners then, so we asked them to tea to Woronzow Road, where we lived. As G.B.S. didn't drink tea, Mrs. Shaw came half an hour before the sage, and the two of them ate bread and salt in the O'Casey home. At all other times, the invitation came from Mrs. Shaw. I like the conceit of St.Jay when he says that if I had been asked to W.Court he would have been asked too to provide the conversation! This shows some of the measure of the man. Without him, there would be silence. Well, at all times, between Shaw and me no words were needed; we were one on most questions; I believe on all. But it is singular that I should be asserting to St.Jay that I actually did visit Shaw.

Even if St.Jay wished to separate me from Shaw's friendship, he might at least have allowed me the privilege of knocking at his door. But I'd like to know what he meant in the implication of "Shaw's kindnesses," as applicable to me. Perhaps you might ask him.

I don't think Fox's book on Jim Larkin worth a damn. I was asked to review it, but refused, because I dislike the man, and I might not have been fair to him. There's a young lad, an American, who is writing a Life of Larkin, and I think this book will be a far, far finer one. He has secured all the official reports of Jim's trial in the U.S.A., when Larkin defended himself, and he tells me they are amazing. He was here with me several times, and he is, I believe, a fine lad. To me, Fox hasn't the gift of writing; and, if he has, he hasn't got the guts to use the gift. St.Jay is, though not in the first class in fancy or imagination, I'm afraid, but forcible, though too dogmatic. His book on Shaw, in my opinion, is a fine biography, and a great tribute to Shaw.

Letter from Shaw to Lady Gregory, [?] June 1928 [sent in envelope dated 22 January, 1958 by Sean O'Casey to Ron Ayling].

Why do you and W.B.Y. treat O'Casey as a baby? Starkie was right, you should have done the play anyhow. Sean is now hors concours. It is literally a hell of a play; but it will clearly force its way on to the stage and Yeats should have submitted to it as a calamity imposed on him by the Act of God, if he could not welcome it as another *Juno*. Besides, he was most extraordinarily wrong about it on the facts. The first act is not a bit realistic; it is deliberately fantastic chanted poetry. This is intensified to a climax in to the second act. Then comes a ruthless return for the last two acts to the fiercest ironic realism. But that is so like Yeats. Give him a job with which you feel sure he will play Bunthorne and he will astonish you with his unique cleverness and subtlety.

Give him one which any second-rater could manage with credit and it is likely as not he will make an appalling mess of it. He has certainly fallen in up to the neck over O'C.

I was looking up a date in *Story of the Abbey Theatre* by Peter Kavanagh, brother to Pat K. the poet. It was printed and published in the U.S.A. and never published here. I seem to remember you asking me about Shaw's letter to Lady Greg., and maybe this is the one you were seeking.

S.O'C.

This letter itself should shew to St. John E. some friendliness towards me.

The London Mercury, 1929.

The *Silver Tassie* is a great play. Its subject is Humanity suffering in the War and Mr. O'Casey treats his subject bitterly, cruelly and greatly. There are two acts that anyone can understand, the first act in which Harry Heegan, champion footballer, wins the Silver Tassie for his club, and departs to the war; and the third in which Harry Heegan, crippled for life, sees his girl leave for a man who is whole and sound. Anyone can see the bitterness of that and the cruelty of the thing that made it happen. Any dramatist, almost, could have made something out of the story. It is a moving, bitter story in itself, and bound to make an audience feel, however remotely and indirectly, that war is a horrible thing. But Mr. O'Casey goes further, miles further. His second act is not devoted to saying that war is horrible. It is devoted to showing what war is, and leaving the audience to judge for itself. The act is solemn portrayal of modern war in which tightly-packed little groups of automatic mole-like men move backwards and forwards in the half-darkness, chanting in plain-song about the bloodiness of the Tommy's lot, about the beastliness of mud and vermin and death and shells and bullets, about the desirability of the Old Kent Road. The scene itself is a dark, shadowy patch of desolation, a waste land indeed, where a church is shattered to ruins, where men are tied to gun-wheels, where the wayside crucifix hangs head downwards, splintered and torn, and where the only source of comfort, the only object of veneration, the only help in the hour of death and destruction, the only strong, unbroken thing, standing outlined against the faint dawn in the sky, is the silhouette of the Great Howitzer.

The Sunday Chronicle, Manchester, 3rd November, 1929.

G.B.S. Unrecognised

You'd think everybody would recognise such a figure as Mr. George Bernard Shaw at sight. He has probably been photographed as much as any man in the country. With his tall lean figure and defiant white beard he commands attention.

Yet at Sean O'Casey's play *The Silver Tassie* the other evening I stood shoulder to shoulder with him in the corridor during one of the intervals.

Dozens of people passed him but not one whispered "There's Bernard Shaw." They didn't recognise him.

A Great Brain

Mr. Shaw was talking animatedly with a friend to whom he was saying that he considered O'Casey a man of genius. "A man with a great brain" was one phrase he used.

The author gratefully acknowledges permission from the following sources to reprint material in their control:

Century Hutchinson for material from *I Had Almost Forgotten* by C. B. Cochran.

Colin Smythe Limited on behalf of the copyright holders, Anne de Winton and Catherine Kennedy, for letters of Lady Gregory.

The Society of Authors on behalf of the St. John Ervine Estate, for St. John Ervine's letter to Ron Ayling, copyright © 1989, The Estate of St. John Ervine.

Jonathan Cape Limited, for letters of T. E. Lawrence from *The Letters of T. E. Lawrence* edited by David Garnett.

The Yale Committee on Literary Propriety, for letter from Eugene O'Neill.

The Society of Authors on behalf of the Bernard Shaw Estate, for letters of George Bernard Shaw, copyright © 1989, The Estate of Bernard Shaw.

The Trustees of the Will of Mrs. Bernard Shaw, for letters of Charlotte Shaw.

Oxford University Press for letter from William Butler Yeats, published in *The Collected Letters of W. B. Yeats* edited by John Kelly and Eric Domville.

The author has made every effort to contact the owners of copyrighted material. So that changes can be made in later printings, omissions or errors should be called to the attention of Charles Scribner's Sons, 866 Third Avenue, New York, NY 10022.

· 143 ·